Praise for *Retired Widow*

"*Retire Widowed: Reclaiming Retirement Security and Peace of Mind After Loss* covers a topic seldom discussed in books about retirement or bereavement—what happens when a spouse passes before or shortly after retirement... Newly bereaved retirees need this book. Its mix of practical financial information, necessary revisions, and emotional support gives voice to many underlying assumptions and precedents most books about widowhood don't tackle."

—D. Donovan, Midwest Book Review Sr. Reviewer

"Professional anecdotes from clients and personal insight make McGray's writing both informative and intimate, covering topics like how to make decisions amid grief to updating estate plans and generating income that works for one, not two. Her advice builds confidence while pinpointing the obligations that accompany the death of a spouse, and she explains even the most daunting issues in straightforward terms. Whether assessing credit cards in your spouse's name, handling auto loans, or determining tax brackets, readers will find a wealth of helpful information to guide them through rebuilding after what McGray terms one of the most destabilizing experiences to face."

—BookLife Review

"A compassionate and practical guide for individuals navigating one of life's most emotionally and financially difficult transitions. The book addresses widowhood with both sensitivity and clarity... What stands out most is the balance between emotional support and practical retirement insight... the book thoughtfully connects both realities, acknowledging how deeply intertwined emotional healing and financial security can become after loss... an important resource for widowed individuals looking for direction, encouragement, and a clearer sense of control over their future during a challenging stage of life."

—KATHY BENNET, Goodreads Reviewer

RETIRE WIDOWED

RETIRE WIDOWED

Reclaiming Retirement Security and Peace of Mind After Loss

TERRI McGRAY, CFP®, AIF®

PRECOCITY PRESS

Editor: Jon Harrison
Creative Director and Book Designer: Susan Shankin
Cover Designer: Sonia Horne
Published by Precocity Press, Los Angeles, CA

ISBN: 979-8-9941476-9-6 (Hardcover)
ISBN: 979-8-9931150-2-3 (Trade paperback)
ISBN: 979-8-9941476-2-7 (eBook)
Library of Congress Control Number: 2026902355
First edition printed in the United States of America

This material is provided for informational and educational purposes only and should not be construed as personalized legal, tax, investment, or financial advice. Readers are encouraged to consult their own qualified attorneys, tax professionals, and financial advisors regarding their individual circumstances before making any decisions.

Any investment strategies discussed are presented for educational purposes only and involve risk, including the potential loss of principal. Past performance is not indicative of future results, and there is no assurance that any investment strategy or recommendation discussed will ultimately be successful or suitable for any specific individual.

Case studies and client examples are hypothetical or have been modified to protect the privacy of individuals. Names, details, and scenarios may have been changed or adapted for illustrative purposes.

While this content discusses estate planning concepts such as wills, trusts, and powers of attorney, it does not constitute legal advice, nor does it replace the need for consultation with a qualified estate planning attorney.

This information is intended for educational purposes only and should not be construed as a recommendation to buy or sell any specific product.

Annuities may be appropriate for some investors depending on their individual financial goals, time horizon, and risk tolerance. Clients should consult with a qualified advisor or insurance professional before making any decisions.

All information is believed to be accurate at the time of publication but may be subject to change without notice.

Longevity Capital Management LLC is a Registered Investment Adviser registered with the U.S. Securities and Exchange Commission ("SEC").

For those who refuse to let loss be the final word.

Contents

Introduction

When Plans Change

Jenny poured two cups of coffee, just like she had every morning for the past 25 years.

Only this morning, one cup sat untouched.

She and Brian had mapped it all out together, side by side. They were going to downsize their home so they could travel more. Jenny was planning to do volunteer work at her local church while Brian was going to mentor at the Boys and Girls Club. She pictured exploring national parks and spending summers on the lake with their grandkids. They had saved diligently, talked through their "someday" dreams, and stayed up late with spreadsheets and calculators, checking to be sure their numbers added up to afford the lake house and their long-awaited trip to Italy.

Throughout her adult life, Jenny and Brian had made decisions as a team. Every stage of her life since college, including raising kids, changing jobs, navigating relocations, buying and selling homes, and caring for her aging parents, was shaped by their shared goals and mutual compromises. Even the tough stuff. When Jenny was diagnosed with breast cancer, Brian drove her to every single doctor's visit. When the Great Recession hit and they had to short sell their house, they worked together, finding strength in each other through that difficult time. When Brian lost his job shortly after their first child was born, they powered through it. It was manageable because they had each other. They navigated life *together*. They found strength as a team and even managed to laugh through their crises. Jenny remembers crying from laughing so hard when Brian surprised her by shaving his head during her chemo treatments. He leaned in when she leaned out. And vice versa.

When it came to retirement, she didn't just imagine financial freedom, she assumed togetherness. It was going to be a second act but this time, on their terms. The kids were grown, and now it was their time for slower mornings and days with the grandkids. Maybe she would finally turn that painting hobby of hers into something more. She and Brian had a rhythm. They had a shared vision. A plan. And it wasn't just about income or investments. It was about companionship, continuity, and shared joy. Every plan they made had two names on it.

She handled the budget, and Brian handled their investments. That's just the way it evolved. She can't quite recall when it started or how they ended up dividing their financial tasks, but that's how it was. Of course, each always checked in with the other before making the big calls. They both knew how to delegate, when to compromise, and where the other's values shaped the family's direction. And now that they were fast approaching retirement, their entire plan, both financial and emotional, was designed for their togetherness.

And then one day everything changed.

It was an ordinary summer evening, like so many others before it. They had eaten dinner together. Brian grilled salmon while they enjoyed a glass of wine, watching the sunset. Soft music played while they ate and chatted about their youngest, who was about to get married.

Later, Brian settled into his favorite chair to watch TV while Jenny tidied up in the kitchen. When he stood up, it happened. A sudden, wrenching pain in his chest. He stumbled, tried to call out, and collapsed before he could take another step. By the time the paramedics arrived, there was nothing they could do. The doctors later explained it was an aortic rupture—a tear so swift, so catastrophic, that even if he had been in the emergency room when it happened, the outcome would probably have been the same.

One moment, he was there, full of life and full of plans. The next, he was gone, along with the future they had planned together. All of it. Vanished in an instant.

Whether your loss was sudden or came after a long illness, nothing truly prepares you for the shattering reality of becoming widowed, especially in retirement, when it's just the two of you. Life without your partner can feel suspended in silence so heavy it leaves you aching for sound. Retirement is meant to be a time of comfort, connection, and ease. But instead of sharing that time together, you suddenly have to navigate a path you never expected.

This book was written for that path. For you.

I started working in the retirement space back in 1988, and over the years I've walked alongside many surviving spouses, helping them navigate both the emotional and financial aftermath of loss.

I'll never forget a story shared at a conference I attended years ago, where the keynote speaker was Dr. Tony Campolo, a respected Baptist pastor who would later become a spiritual advisor to President Bill Clinton. He spoke candidly about losing his wife. After the funeral, he and his three sons walked out of the church and sat quietly on the steps. Breaking the silence, he said, "Boys, this is exactly how I wanted it to be." They looked at him, confused. Then he gently explained, "I didn't want to leave her behind to feel this pain."

Those words have stayed with me because in the end no one wants their partner to suffer the heartbreak of loss. But for those left behind, that void becomes very real, and so do the financial decisions that follow.

Still, with time, care, and the right support, it's possible to move forward. There is strength in remembering the love that shaped you. There is power in reclaiming your sense of direction. And there is hope in the search for peace. Your future is in your hands.

I've written *Retired Widowed* for those who are approaching or already in retirement and now find themselves navigating life alone. It's for the newly widowed staring at stacks of paperwork, unsure which accounts are in whose name, what income will continue, or how to make financial decisions without the person they once made every decision with. It's for those who suddenly need to rethink not just their finances, but their entire future. And most of all it's for the surviving spouses who feel overwhelmed by grief while trying to make sense of Social Security, close out accounts, meet with attorneys and financial professionals, and make a series of irreversible financial decisions. This book is here to help you do that, one step at a time.

I've worked with widowed clients for over three decades. I've witnessed the chaos and confusion that often follows loss. No matter how prepared one may have thought they were, losing a spouse is one of the most destabilizing experiences to face—emotionally, mentally, and financially. I've seen women who hadn't written a check in years suddenly responsible for managing multimillion-dollar portfolios. I've seen men overwhelmed by everyday tasks their spouses once handled, from paying household bills to preparing meals. It doesn't matter how educated, accomplished, or financially savvy you are. The truth is, when you lose your partner you can be left feeling completely adrift.

Sadly though, this is part of the human experience. As painful as it is, loss is something most all married couples will eventually face. Death is a heartbreaking reality of life, and while it may feel deeply personal and isolating, it is also universal. You are not alone in this even if you feel very alone right now.

Psychological research consistently shows that the loss of a spouse is one of the most devastating life events a human being can endure. It is often ranked as more stressful than the loss of a parent, a job, or even one's own health. The grief that follows is not just emotional. The despair, the brain fog, the exhaustion are all normal. And while it may not feel like it now, over time, the intensity of the pain will begin to ease.

Intellectually of course you knew that one of you would live longer. But knowing it in theory doesn't dull the sharp edge of living it in reality. You reasonably assumed you would enjoy retirement as a team, so when the foundation you built together suddenly disappears, it's normal to feel as if the ground beneath you has crumbled.

While it seems as if everything that was certain has come undone, I can assure you resilience has already begun to take root. It's okay if you don't feel strong right now. Grief has a way of making us feel unmoored. But picking up this book is a testament to your courage, a small yet significant act of resilience. Trust that strength will come.

In every client who has experienced this kind of loss, I've seen strength they did not know they had. I've seen the clarity that returns one decision at a time. And the quiet resilience that helps them rebuild a life that is different but still meaningful. It may not be the life you planned, but it can still be one filled with purpose, peace, and even joy. You are not starting over; you are starting *forward*.

Unfortunately, though, the financial services industry falls short in recognizing how intertwined money is with grief. You're not just having to make financial decisions; you're having to make them in the shadow of trauma. At a time when you're emotionally vulnerable, you're expected to think logically, calculate risks, and make permanent decisions that impact the rest of your life.

So I'm writing about what financial books overlook. This book is not simply about assets, taxes, and retirement planning. It's about identity, safety, memory, and legacy. It's about regaining a sense of control when everything around you feels uncertain.

And yes, it is about survival, both emotionally and financially.

THE MYTH OF THE SMOOTH RETIREMENT

We are sold a myth of retirement as a peaceful glide into the golden years, filled with big smiles, lazy morning walks, and maybe a little golf or travel. And while people do find this kind of joy in retirement, few are prepared for how quickly the script can change. The truth is retirement rarely unfolds exactly as planned. Health issues, financial uncertainty, and loss can upend even the most carefully constructed financial plan.

And widowhood is one of the most overlooked transitions in retirement. The majority of women over age 65 will outlive their spouses. According to the US Census Bureau, approximately 32 percent of women aged 65 and older are widowed, compared to just 11 percent of men.

The numbers grow even starker with age. Fifty-two percent of women between the ages of 75 and 84 are widowed, and that number rises to 76 percent for women over age 85. And if you feel like widowhood came too early in your life, you might be surprised to know that the average age at which women in the United States become widows is just 59. That means many others face this loss long before they, or their retirement plans, are prepared for it. You are not alone.

Widowhood is not just a woman's experience, of course. While fewer men are widowed overall, those who do lose their spouse often face a different set of emotional and logistical challenges. Many men have been deeply reliant on their partner for emotional grounding, daily routines, or managing key aspects of household life. And men tend to be less likely to seek support or discuss their grief openly, which can make the transition feel especially heavy and unsteady.

Losing a spouse is one of life's most profound transitions, yet too few financial plans truly address what happens when one spouse passes away. Being widowed changes your tax status, your income, your housing needs, your investment timeline, your estate plan, and your sense of purpose. Even your daily rhythm shifts in ways you couldn't have imagined. Like Jenny and her morning coffee routine, your married rhythm is wired into your habits and patterns. It doesn't simply disappear when your spouse is gone. But you are no longer living the life you once planned, and you are no longer the same person you were when you planned it. Your needs, goals, and identity have shifted and, ultimately, your financial plan must shift with you.

Some think that by 80 or 90 years of age you're somehow more "prepared" for loss. But in my experience, that's simply not true. Love doesn't fade with age, and neither does the pain of loss. When your partner is gone, routine, security, and often your very sense of self changes no matter what your age. For older retirees, it can be even more difficult because that loss can bring more than just grief. It can bring fear because illness, mobility issues, or cognitive changes can quickly complicate everything. My mother-in-law was struggling with Parkinson's when her husband died. Not only did she have to process the heartbreak of losing him, but she also lost her caregiver, her sense of security, and ultimately, her home. Her grief was compounded by the sudden upheaval of everything familiar, as she had to go into a nursing home. When her beloved husband passed away, her entire world was turned upside down. That kind of change isn't just emotional. It's deeply disorienting.

No matter where you are in life when loss comes, this book is here to help you find your footing again.

RETIREMENT REIMAGINED

This is a book about retirement, and not just the financial aspect. It's also about your time, your energy, your quality of life, and your relationships. In the pages ahead we'll talk about asset preservation and IRA rollovers, income streams and required minimum distributions. And we'll also talk about courage. About rebuilding confidence. About realizing that it's not too late to have a rich life, even if it's not the one you originally envisioned.

According to the 2024 MassMutual Retirement Happiness Study, 67 percent of retirees within their first 15 years of retirement reported being happier since retiring, and 82 percent felt more relaxed on a typical day. This includes single retirees, both those who entered retirement alone and those who became single along the way.

Of course, happiness doesn't happen automatically. Cultivating strong social connections, staying engaged in meaningful activities, and maintaining physical well-being all play a role. While life after loss can feel frightening and unwelcome, experts note that, over time, many people discover new avenues for personal growth, a renewed sense of independence, and a deeper comfort with solitude. This is not about discounting what was lost but finding a way to move on with strength and a different purpose.

Whether you are just starting to find your footing again, or have been rebuilding for some time, it is never too late to create a life of meaning, connection, and peace on your terms.

In *Retire Widowed,* you'll read about:

- how to make smart decisions when you're emotionally raw
- what to do (and what not to do) in the first 30, 60, and 90 days
- how to update your estate plan so it reflects your new priorities
- when to sell, when to hold, and when to walk away
- how to create an income plan that works for one, not two
- how to handle the tax changes that come with widowhood, including the so-called "widow's penalty"
- how to protect your future from predators, poor advice, and costly missteps
- how to rebuild your retirement one step at a time, with clarity and confidence for what comes next

Before we get into the planning, however, we begin with recognition. That's because before you can chart a new course, you must acknowledge where you are. You must acknowledge what's been lost, not just your partner but the life you envisioned together. The plans you made. The familiar rhythm of your days. And with that loss often comes a flood of emotions you never expected to navigate while trying to make critical financial decisions.

It's okay to admit that you didn't want to do this alone. In fact, it's okay to be angry. This isn't what you worked so hard to face. You planned for freedom, but with companionship. So it's only natural to feel cheated, heartbroken, or even furious. Yell. Cry. Pound the floor. Hug the pillow. Every reaction is valid. It's all part of how we process a future that no longer looks anything like the one you imagined.

Maybe your loss is still fresh, and you're just beginning to come up for air. Or maybe the worst of the grief has passed, and you're ready, albeit tentatively, cautiously, to start rebuilding. Wherever you are, this is the right place to begin. This book is not here to rush you. It's here to meet you, support you, and walk beside you as you take the next step, in your own time, in your own way.

If you feel exhausted, it's normal. If you're not just tired, but soul-deep weary, it's normal. If you are drained from all the decisions, the emotions, the endless list of things that suddenly fell on your shoulders, it's normal. Grief is exhausting. So is dealing with the mounds of paperwork. So is putting on a brave face when you're not sure how you'll get through the day. If you find yourself forgetting things, feeling numb, or just wanting to stay in bed, it's okay. Allow yourself time to rest. If your loss is fresh, allow your body to set the pace. You're not broken. You're human. Rest if you need to. Breathe. Give yourself permission to pause. Healing takes energy, and right now it's okay if you don't have much to spare.

It's also normal to feel overwhelmed by responsibilities you never expected to face alone. Grief makes even simple tasks feel impossible. Your brain is in overdrive just trying to process the loss, making it hard to think clearly about finances, housing, or legal matters. Grief isn't just emotional. It's physical. It clouds your focus, drains your energy, and distorts time. One moment you're handling paperwork, the next you're staring into space. That's not failure. That's grief. And it's why self-compassion matters now more than ever.

You may feel guilty for not being more prepared, or even for surviving. You might feel relief that their pain is over, that caregiving has ended or that the house is quieter. And then, just when you don't expect it, joy or laughter sneaks in. And you wonder if it's too soon. You might question whether you're grieving the "right" way. But there is no right way. Grief is messy. It loops, it fades, and then it returns. Feeling grief, guilt, gratitude, even hope and happiness isn't wrong. It's healing.

There's no script for this. No perfect timeline. What you're feeling is *human.* You're allowed to take your time, feel what you feel, and move forward at your own pace. The key, though, is to begin. Granted, some days will be productive and others paralyzing. Some choices will bring closure, others new waves of emotion. So give yourself time, space, and grace without pressure. When you're ready, you can rebuild, and on your terms.

But remember, this is your life. You decide what comes next. Don't let the weeks, months, or years slip by without reflecting, planning, or taking steps forward. It's okay if you don't have the energy to map everything out right now. However, just begin with one step. Don't worry, though, we will take it together.

A PERSONAL NOTE

I didn't write this book from a distance. I've helped hundreds of widows and widowers navigate life after loss. I've walked beside them through estate administration, downsizing a home, adjusting cash flow, and making sense of unfamiliar investment portfolios. More importantly, I've listened. I've sat with their fears, heard their questions, and witnessed their quiet moments of resilience.

This is your life now. It may not be the life you planned, but it is still yours to shape. This book is your guide to help you make it happen. A new life is awaiting you. A life to be shaped not by what you've lost, but by what you still have to live, give, and become. Remember, you are not starting over. You are starting again, carrying with you the wisdom you've earned and the strength you've uncovered. Let what comes next begin not with fear, but with possibility.

Although your spouse is no longer here to walk beside you, they are still part of the journey. If they could tell you anything now, it would be to keep going. Carry their memory not as a weight, but as a light to guide you. Enrich the lives of your children and grandchildren, your friends and extended family with your presence, your laughter, your love, and your wisdom. Life is still a gift. And your spouse would have wanted you to unwrap it with courage, strength, and hope.

Millions of others have walked this path, including, most likely, your own mother or father. This pain, while deeply personal, is also a part of life's fabric. It's something we never want to face, yet a meaningful life still lies ahead of you. Moving forward isn't about forgetting the past. It's about honoring it while stepping into the future with courage.

That includes your financial life. As a newly single person, how you manage your income, investments, and estate plan will shape what comes next for you. This is about more than money, of course. It's about making decisions that support your goals, your independence, and your peace of mind. This is an important time to align your financial life with your values and your needs, and to do so at a pace that feels right for you.

That means there is no need to rush. You need not have all the answers today. However, you do need a place to begin. And that's where we'll start here, together. *Retire Widowed* will help you begin. Thoughtfully. Practically. One step at a time. You didn't choose this path, but you can choose what you do with it, and I'm here to help you walk it toward stability, strength, and a future that brings you peace, purpose, and joy.

CHAPTER ONE

Navigating the Storm

How to Make Smart Decisions When You're Emotionally Raw

You were my once in a lifetime.
And now, you are my always.

Grief begins with love. And that's what makes this loss so overwhelming. Yet, with time and care, you will find your footing again. While the journey through grief is profoundly individual, it also marks the beginning of a new chapter. From here the focus turns to rebuilding, as you begin to navigate the emotional, practical, and financial realities that follow loss. The aim is to help you regain a sense of control, purpose, and confidence as you move forward.

When a spouse dies, life changes in an instant. Yet even as you're trying to catch your breath, the world keeps moving. Funeral plans. Financial accounts. Social Security. Health insurance. Decisions need to be made, ready or not. It helps to know what truly needs your attention and what can wait. There's no need to dive into every detail or solve everything at once. But there are a few essential tasks that, unfortunately, can't be delayed.

Start by gathering multiple certified copies of the death certificate. It is generally recommended that you order 10 to 15, since you'll need them to handle everything from bank accounts to insurance claims. Next, notify Social Security, your spouse's employer (if applicable), and any pension administrator. If your spouse was receiving benefits, those payments will stop, and survivor benefits may need to be initiated.

If funeral or memorial arrangements haven't yet been completed, this can feel incredibly difficult without a plan in place. In that case, lean on family, close friends, or a funeral director to help carry some of the burden. If your spouse was a veteran, you may be eligible for burial benefits or military honors, and the funeral home can guide you in accessing those resources.

Beyond immediate notifications, take steps to safeguard the home and estate. That may mean changing the locks if caregivers had access and securing valuables, especially in situations where family dynamics or outsiders such as movers or service providers no longer need entry. Other tasks like cancelling subscriptions, updating automatic payments, and notifying credit card companies can wait a few more days, but should be added to a simple checklist so they don't get overlooked. When you're overwhelmed, even crossing off one small task can bring a sense of progress and control.

As you move through these essential tasks, a difficult emotional hurdle that may begin to surface is the sense of isolation. In the early days you may be surrounded by the support of family, friends, and even acquaintances offering condolences. But as time passes you may notice that friends and family, as caring as they are, must return to their own routines. The house may grow quieter. The meals and calls taper off. And in that stillness your grief may feel sharper.

Your body or mind might urge you to lie down. You may feel paralyzed. That's normal. Grief has its own rhythm. And on those days, remember that progress doesn't have to be dramatic. Making a phone call, gathering a document, or getting dressed is enough. Small steps matter, because each one helps steady you. Over time, the weight of grief shifts. It won't disappear, but it will get less paralyzing, leaving space for strength and, eventually, a measure of peace.

After Judy lost her husband of 41 years, she told me it felt like the walls were closing in. The first week or two was a blur of visitors, phone calls, and sympathy cards. By the third week, though, the house was quiet. Her adult children had returned to their homes. Friends stopped checking in as frequently. She found herself staring out the window, unsure of what to do next and unsure who she could talk to without feeling like a burden.

Judy had always been strong and independent. She was the type who handled things without asking for help. But grief was different. It left her unsteady. She said to me, "I thought I was supposed to be okay by now. But I'm not. I feel like I'm floating."

Eventually, with a little encouragement, she joined a small bereavement group at a local church. It wasn't easy for her to walk in that first day. But she told me that by the end of the hour, she had shared something she hadn't told anyone else. She told them how much she missed hearing her husband breathe beside her in bed. She said that when others in the group nodded, she knew they truly understood. That single moment of being heard, rather than placated by her daughter's quick "I know it's hard, Mom," or feeling guilty for burdening a friend with yet another "poor me" phone call, moved something in her. For the first time, she didn't feel like she had to edit her grief or apologize for how long it was lasting. She felt understood, not managed. And that made all the difference. Judy didn't realize how a group of strangers could offer greater peace and healing than her own friends and family, but over time the support group became her lifeline.

It didn't erase the pain, but it made her feel less alone. And when she later began working one-on-one with a grief counselor, she found new tools to move through each day with a little more strength. Judy didn't just survive those first few months; she began to heal because, in her case, she needed to reach beyond her inner circle for the kind of support her friends and family simply couldn't provide.

If you feel stuck or simply need more help, professional help such as counseling or therapy can be invaluable. A trained professional can offer guidance and tools to navigate the complex emotions you are feeling and, most importantly, help you find a path forward. Of course not everyone feels the need for or wants to reach out for help, but there's no shame in needing support beyond what friends and family can offer. If you find yourself having thoughts you don't want to share with others close to you, or reactions that catch you off guard, don't be afraid or embarrassed to seek support. You are navigating a very difficult situation. Remember, healing doesn't mean forgetting your spouse, but it also doesn't mean moving through life feeling hollow or detached.

Some widows find comfort in group counseling or bereavement groups, where they're surrounded by others who truly understand what this kind of loss feels like. Others prefer the privacy and focus of one-on-one support. If you are at a loss, talk to your primary care doctor about what resources might be right for you. For those with a strong spiritual foundation, faith-based counseling or speaking with a trusted clergy member can be equally valuable. Spiritual guidance can offer not only emotional support but also a deeper sense of purpose and peace during a time of profound questioning.

The point is that help is available. Many of our clients have shared that although their kids meant well, they didn't fully grasp the depth of what they were going through. Certainly, sometimes the most meaningful support comes from professionals or those who have walked this road before you. Asking for help is a courageous step toward healing, and even one conversation may help you move forward.

FINANCIAL CONSIDERATIONS: A CORNERSTONE OF STABILITY

Amidst the emotional turmoil, there are practical considerations that must be addressed, and finances are at the forefront. Of course, the loss of a spouse can significantly impact one's financial situation. Whether it's managing the loss of income, handling debts, or understanding new tax implications, the financial landscape can seem as treacherous as the emotional one.

As the fog begins to thin, even just a little, you may find yourself facing questions you never imagined having to answer on your own. Can I stay in this house? Do I have enough income? What happens to our retirement accounts? These aren't just financial questions. They're personal matters, tied to the life you shared and the future you're now left to manage. But facing them is part of your healing process. Financial clarity isn't just about money; it's about restoring a sense of control, independence, and confidence. You don't have to address this all at once. You just need to begin.

Wealth management can become a cornerstone of stability during this time. It isn't about worrying about today's market conditions or chasing investment returns. It's about creating a steady foundation. Developing a smart financial plan is a process that helps you understand what you have, how long it will last, and what is needed to support your life moving forward. When everything else feels like it's shifting beneath your feet, a well-structured financial plan becomes one of the few places where vision and control can be restored.

This is especially true in widowhood, when income streams change, expenses shift, and long-term plans need to be reevaluated. Financial planning brings structure to that process. It helps you to:

- organize your assets and understand how they work together
- make tax-efficient decisions about investment accounts, retirement distributions or inherited accounts
- evaluate what's safe to spend now versus what should be preserved
- reframe your goals around this new phase of life—not based on what was, but on what's still possible

In other words, wealth management becomes a stabilizing force. It won't fix the emotional pain of loss, but it removes unnecessary uncertainty from the financial side of your life. And that space, free of worry and confusion, allows you to focus on healing, rebuilding, and eventually redefining what your retirement can look like now.

Consequently, it is crucial to assess your current financial situation comprehensively. This includes understanding all your assets, liabilities, income sources, and expenses. It will also be necessary to revise your financial and retirement plan to reflect your new reality.

One of the first steps is to gather all essential financial documents, including wills, insurance policies, and bank and investment statements. Having a clear picture of your financial condition is the foundation upon which to build a new plan. Consulting with a financial advisor can bring greater efficiency and provide meaningful, productive direction to your process. They can help in creating a revised budget, building a sound investment strategy, and developing a solid plan that aligns with your changed circumstances.

Additionally, understanding the benefits and entitlements available to you is crucial. These may include Social Security benefits, pension plans, and life insurance payouts. You also need to set realistic income goals in order to maintain self-sufficiency throughout your lifetime. Navigating these issues can be complex for any retiree, but after a major life change such as the loss of a spouse, this becomes even more critical. Professional advice can help ensure that nothing important is overlooked.

TAKING YOUR FIRST FINANCIAL INVENTORY

In the early days after loss, financial matters can be overwhelming, especially if your spouse handled most of the money decisions. But even for those who were involved in their finances, everything can feel suddenly unfamiliar. Remember, this isn't about solving everything at once. It's simply about understanding where you stand in the wake of this change.

Taking an initial financial inventory is like turning on the lights in a dark room. You may not know yet what's in every corner, but you need to begin to see what is there. And from there you can make thoughtful decisions instead of rushed ones.

Start with the essentials:

1. Identify All Income Sources

What money is still coming in each month? This could include:

- Social Security. You will lose his or her benefit if they were collecting one, but you may be entitled to a survivor benefit, which could even replace your own if it's higher.
- Pension or retirement income. Some pensions continue payments to a surviving spouse; others do not.

- Required Minimum Distributions (RMDs). If your spouse was over 73, these may apply to inherited retirement accounts.
- Investment income. Interest, dividends, or scheduled distributions that could be subject to different tax rates now.
- Annuities. If you were listed as a beneficiary or joint annuitant, distribution options needs to be reviewed and carefully considered.
- Life insurance. This may include employer-sponsored and private policies.

If you're unsure whether an income source continues or stops after death, don't guess—verify. Even a small, missed detail could have a lasting impact. Taking the time to confirm these details is not just about protecting your finances; it's also a way to regain a sense of control. In the early stages of grief, when so much feels uncertain, even small acts of progress can bring relief. The process of gathering information and checking off simple tasks may feel like busywork, but it's productive and can be healing. It keeps you moving forward.

2. Review Account Ownership and Access

Next, look at how your financial accounts are titled:

- Are they joint, individual, or in a trust?
- Do you have online access and the legal authority to act on all accounts?
- Do beneficiary designations need to be updated where applicable?

In many cases, financial institutions will require a death certificate, which may take a few weeks to arrive. That's okay. This time will allow you to focus on your family and your loss. However, once they arrive, you'll need to gather what you can about your accounts and make a list of any institutions you need to call or visit. If you have a financial advisor, now is the time to speak with them and request a full account summary and beneficiary review.

This process may feel tedious or even emotionally draining, but every form you complete, every call you make, is a step forward. This isn't just about managing paperwork. You're taking back a sense of control when so much feels uncertain. So give yourself credit for what you're handling, even on the hard days, and remember it's okay to go slow if you feel overwhelmed. You're doing more than you may realize.

3. List All Monthly Bills and Automatic Payments

One of the most grounding things you can do in the weeks after loss is to get a handle on what's going out each month. While it may seem like a small detail, understanding your monthly bills and automatic payments is an essential step toward regaining financial control and peace of mind.

Stabilizing your cash flow isn't just about budgeting; it's about avoiding surprises. It helps you avoid missed payments, uncover unnecessary expenses, and start making decisions based on facts rather than fear. Even something as simple as identifying a recurring subscription or a joint account payment can create clarity in a time that feels anything but clear.

Begin tracking:

- mortgage or rent
- utilities (gas, electric, water, phone, internet)
- insurance premiums (auto, home, health, long-term care)
- credit cards or loan payments

- streaming services, memberships, or donation subscriptions
- any lingering medical bills

This is where a notepad, spreadsheet, or personal finance app can be your ally. Keep it simple. One line at a time. And remember, this isn't about solving your entire financial life in a day. It's like creating a foundation, brick by brick.

You may discover services you no longer need or find charges under your spouse's name that require cancellation. Don't worry about perfect organization right away. Just start a list.

4. Locate and Review Important Documents

This step may feel like one of the most difficult, both emotionally and practically. Sorting through documents often means sifting through drawers, files, or digital folders your spouse once managed or tucked away. It can feel intrusive, even painful, like opening a part of their world you never expected to navigate alone. That's okay. Go slowly and allow yourself grace.

Start by pulling together what you can. It's easiest to just begin with the essentials that will help you understand where things stand:

- Your spouse's will or trust documents. These guide what happens next and may provide important legal instructions or identify key people involved in settling the estate.

- Life insurance policies. These may be held privately, through an employer, or bundled inside retirement accounts. Make a note of each one's contact information.

- Most recent tax returns. If you were leaning on your spouse for the finances, a prior-year return provides a roadmap of income sources, assets, deductions, and account locations.

- Bank and investment account statements. Whether paper or digital, these give insight into balances, ownership, and automatic transfers.
- Marriage certificate. Some institutions, particularly Social Security, may require a certified copy to confirm eligibility for survivor benefits.
- Retirement account statements. 401(k)s, IRAs, annuities—each may have different distribution rules for beneficiaries.

If this feels like too much to do alone, don't hesitate to ask for help. A trusted professional, adult child, or close friend can assist you in creating a checklist and working through it one step at a time. And, remember, this doesn't need to be finished in a day. It's a process.

WHAT NOT TO DECIDE YET

By now you may have started to get a clearer view of your financial picture or at least begun gathering the pieces. And with that clarity often comes a sense of urgency. It's common to feel the impulse to do something—anything—to regain control. Maybe you're thinking about selling the house. Or cashing out accounts. Or giving away belongings just to clear the emotional clutter. That's natural. When your world has been turned upside down, making big decisions can feel like a way to create order.

But this is exactly the moment to slow down.

When you're grieving, your perspective is altered. Your tolerance for uncertainty is lower. You may be more susceptible to suggestions or too eager to relieve emotional discomfort by acting too quickly. And unfortunately, financial decisions made during this vulnerable time can have long-term consequences that are hard or impossible to undo.

For example:

- Selling the home may seem like a relief now, but later you might realize you weren't ready to let go of that space—or the equity.
- Cashing in retirement accounts may create unexpected tax liabilities or reduce future income you'll need down the road.
- Changing investments while emotionally overwhelmed could lead to misalignment with your actual goals, risk tolerance, or time horizon.
- Giving away assets to adult children or others might feel generous in the moment, but without a complete financial plan, it may compromise your own security.

None of these choices are wrong in and of themselves. They just need the right timing, the right information, and the right mindset. And none of us have that in the first few weeks or even months after such a painful loss. That's why patience right now isn't procrastination, it's protection. It gives you time to let the dust settle, to process, and to gather the input you need to make confident, not reactive, choices.

If a decision feels urgent, ask yourself:

- Would I still want to do this six months from now?
- Am I doing this to feel better emotionally—or because it's financially sound?
- Have I reviewed this decision with someone objective and experienced?

If the answer is unclear, the best move is often to wait. Time brings perspective. And while clarity may depend on answers, it often begins by asking the right questions.

FAMILY DYNAMICS AFTER LOSS: HEALTHY SUPPORT VS. UNHEALTHY CONTROL

Grief doesn't happen in a vacuum. When a spouse dies, family members often step in. Sometimes they step in to help, sometimes they step in to manage, and sometimes, without meaning to, they step in to take over. You may find yourself relying more on your adult children or extended family during this time, and that can be a source of great comfort. But it can also introduce new complications, especially if boundaries aren't clear or if emotional roles shift too quickly.

And in the middle of all this, you may not see what's really happening, especially when you're emotionally raw.

When Support Is Healthy

In healthy grieving environments, family members step in with compassion and respect. They offer help, but don't pressure you. They give you room to make decisions, even if you're moving slowly. They ask what you need instead of assuming. And while they may express concern, they trust your capacity to process, to decide, and to heal in your own time.

Here's what healthy support might look like:

- A child who says, *I'm here if you need help going through Dad's paperwork, but only when you're ready.*
- A sibling who checks in regularly, not just about tasks, but asks about how you're really doing.
- A family member who offers to drive you to the lawyer's office or sit with you at the bank, without inserting their own agenda.
- Conversations that *include* you—not that are *about* you.

Healthy support empowers. It doesn't replace your voice. It reinforces it. When you receive it, it's a gift, and it should be seen that way. If you have even one person in your life that shows up in this way, who respects your pace and stands beside you rather than in front of you, hold that close because that kind of support is not something to take for granted. It's one of the quiet blessings that can carry you through the hardest parts of this journey.

But not everyone has that. Some people don't have children. Some have family members who are absent, or the relationship is strained, or who aren't able to provide the kind of support needed. I've walked beside clients who had no one—who grieved in isolation, made every phone call themselves, and built a new life from the ground up with no hand to hold.

If that's you, your path may be lonelier, but it is no less worthy of support. Help can come in different forms. It can come through a trusted advisor, a therapist, a grief group, a church community, or even an unsuspecting friend. If you don't have a built-in support system, you're not without options. It simply means you'll need to be more intentional about building one.

HOW TO BUILD YOUR OWN TEAM

If you don't have children, close family, or friends you feel comfortable leaning on, you are not alone, although it might feel that way. You don't need a crowd. You just need two or three thoughtful, trustworthy individuals who can help you make decisions, think clearly, and move forward without feeling so alone.

Here are a few places to start:

1. A Financial Advisor Who Understands Widowhood

You need more than investment advice right now. You need someone who can listen, explain without pressure, and help you make smart financial decisions—at your pace, not theirs. A qualified advisor can help you clarify your income sources, avoid unnecessary mistakes, and organize the pieces of your financial life in a way that feels manageable. But at a time like this developing trust with someone new can feel like one more emotional hill to climb.

You and your spouse may have worked with a financial advisor for many years. That connection can be an important source of stability now. A trusted advisor not only understands your financial picture but also the context behind it—your goals, values, and the decisions you made together over the years. In a time when so much feels uncertain, that continuity matters. Having someone who can help you prioritize, break things into manageable steps, and act as a steady hand can relieve some of the pressure. It's not just about the numbers. It's about having an ally to help you move forward with care and confidence.

On the other hand, if the advisor primarily worked with your spouse and is someone you barely know or perhaps have never met, you may feel conflicted. Some advisors are excellent at guiding surviving spouses and can make the process more thoughtful and supportive. Others may treat you as if you're simply stepping into your spouse's seat, without truly taking the time to understand who you are or what you need. Don't feel pressured to keep working with them simply out of loyalty or convenience. However, give it time and see if the relationship feels respectful, inclusive, and focused on your future. Ask yourself, *do they speak in clear language? Do they ask thoughtful questions? Do they make you feel capable and in control? Or overwhelmed and small?*

If you don't feel a connection or sense of alignment, you're not obligated to continue that relationship. In fact, one of the greatest steps you can take is to evaluate whether your current advisors are the right fit, and how to find the professionals that you need who truly understand what you're facing now.

You deserve to be heard, supported, and guided with care and competence. Whether that's with someone you've known for years or someone new, the right advisor will earn your trust by meeting you where you are.

2. An Estate or Elder Law Attorney

Even if you and your spouse had a will or trust, it's still critical to have a legal professional review your current documents when your family structure and financial responsibilities have changed. An estate or elder law attorney can help you understand what's required to settle your spouse's affairs, ensure everything is titled correctly, and guide you in updating your own estate plan so it reflects your new reality.

But let's be honest: working with an attorney in the midst of grief can feel intimidating. And if you don't have one that you have already connected with, you may feel like you're walking into a stranger's office.

If that attorney makes you feel respected, included, and clearly explains what's happening and why, you will likely find great comfort in working with them. Some lawyers are just technically skilled, while others are also compassionate professionals who know how to handle your loss with care and professionalism. If that's the case, let them be a resource to you.

But if you feel rushed, talked down to, or ignored, you are not obligated to keep working with someone just because your spouse did or just because they wrote your trust years ago. This is your life now, and your legal team should support your confidence, not chip away at it.

A good estate or elder law attorney can also help you to:

- retitle property in your name
- discuss beneficiary designation options for your accounts, retirement plans and insurance policies

- review or revise your will, trust, and powers of attorney
- provide guidance if you don't have family or want to name someone neutral to act on your behalf
- help you understand whether probate is necessary, and if so, how to navigate it
- protect your estate from avoidable taxes, delays, or conflicts

If you don't have an attorney you trust, ask your financial advisor, CPA, or another professional for a referral. Look for someone who specializes in estate planning or elder law. Ideally you will find someone who regularly works with those who have lost a spouse, and who speaks to you like a person, not a case file.

Just like with financial advisors, the right legal support isn't just about credentials. It's about chemistry, transparency, and care. Don't worry if you don't have all the answers or everything together; in fact, that's what your attorney is there for. Their job is to help you understand what you need, your options, ask the right questions on your behalf, and make sure you're protected as you take your next steps forward.

3. A CPA or Tax Professional

When your spouse dies, taxes are often the last thing on your mind, but they shouldn't be ignored for long. Filing that first tax return as a widow can be confusing, especially if your spouse always handled the financial details or if your household relied heavily on their income, benefits, or pension. This is where the right CPA or tax professional can make a real difference.

If you and your spouse had an established relationship with a trusted tax professional, now is the time to lean on that connection. They already know your situation, understand your filing status, and are familiar with the unique details of your income and financial history. That kind of continuity can be a relief when so much else feels uncertain. They can help you move forward with confidence and care.

But if the CPA worked mainly with your spouse and was someone you barely knew or never dealt with directly, you might feel unsure about whether to keep working with them. That hesitation is valid. A good tax professional, just like a good attorney or financial advisor, should be able to guide you without condescension, explain decisions in plain language, and listen closely to your evolving needs. If that's not the case, look elsewhere. This is your financial life now, and you deserve someone who will treat you with care and respect.

In some cases, this might be the first time in years you've filed taxes as an individual. You may be facing changes in deductions, capital gains, or the so-called "widow's tax penalty" which is an increase in tax burden that can surprise many surviving spouses. A qualified tax professional can help you navigate these changes and think proactively about things like estimated taxes, inherited accounts, or the timing of withdrawals.

The right professional will not only help you file taxes accurately but will also look ahead and help you avoid unnecessary burdens. The goal is to make sure your financial picture continues to support your goals in retirement.

4. A Therapist, Grief Counselor, or Spiritual Leader

Your emotional health matters just as much as your financial stability. Grief isn't just a feeling, it's a process, and it doesn't move in a straight line. Whether you turn to a licensed therapist, a clergy member, or a local grief support group, having someone who can listen without judgment or an agenda can be grounding. If you need a space where you can say the things you're afraid to say elsewhere, where you don't have to be "okay," where someone knows how to sit with your pain without rushing to fix it, a skilled therapist or grief counselor can help you sort through difficult emotions like guilt, regret, fear, or even anger, and they can be an important part of your support team.

If you're a person of faith, then a spiritual leader, your pastor, priest, rabbi, or chaplain can be a deeply comforting presence. Many religious communities also offer grief ministries or structured support groups that are welcoming, encouraging, and spiritually aligned with your values.

5. A Practical Ally or Peer

A supporter could be a neighbor, friend, fellow church member, or even someone from a widow's group. I've had clients tell me people they barely knew reached out to them unexpectedly, or they reached out to friends or neighbors who they had previously only waved to over the years or exchanged a few words with in passing. But during their time of loss, these people stepped in and offered real support. They accompanied them to appointments, helped sort through paperwork, and sat beside them with a cup of coffee and no need to fill the silence. They did not try to fix anything or offer advice. They were simply present. And sometimes that is everything.

Practical companionship doesn't require deep history or emotional intimacy. It just requires presence, patience, and kindness. In fact, some of the most healing support comes not from those closest to you, but from people who are willing to walk with you without expectations.

And you may not realize it, but you are not the only one who feels alone right now. The person you reach out to, whether it is a neighbor, an old friend, or someone sitting near you at church, may also be longing for connection. If there's a person who has come to mind as you've read this, consider picking up the phone.

Invite them to coffee. Ask if they'd like to take a walk or sit with you while you go through a stack of paperwork. The truth is many people want to help. They just don't know they're needed until you ask.

HOW TO START BUILDING YOUR CIRCLE

One of the best ways to move forward in a healthy, productive way is to build a solid team. And the first step is often the most difficult. Perhaps the best place to start is to begin by identifying the gaps: Where do you feel uncertain? Who do you already know that you trust? What kind of help do you need most? Is it emotional, financial, logistical? Then, take one step. Schedule a consultation, ask for a recommendation, attend a local event, or reach out to someone who offered, "If you ever need anything…" and take them up on it.

When Concern Turns Controlling

In the weeks and months after losing a spouse, it's natural to feel overwhelmed, and just as natural to welcome help from those who care about you. Many people genuinely want to ease your burden and protect you from making difficult decisions alone. But sometimes, in their effort to be helpful, boundaries can begin to blur.

What starts as care or concern can quietly shift into control. Maybe your adult child insists on managing all your finances "so you do not have to think about it." A stepchild starts questioning every purchase you make. A friend urges you to sell your home, convinced it is "too much for you now." These suggestions may be well-intended, but when they begin to override your autonomy, minimize your grief, or make you feel guilty for needing space to process, they can become problematic.

Unfortunately, in a vulnerable moment, this kind of overreach can be hard to spot. You may feel relieved to hand over some responsibility or grateful that someone is "taking charge." But if you begin to feel uneasy, dismissed, or pressured, it's important to pause and take a closer look. Your voice, your timing, and your decisions still matter. Because you are vulnerable, you may not recognize the shift in control.

Red flags to watch for:

- Pressure to make major financial decisions before you are ready.
- Being discouraged from speaking with your own advisor or attorney.
- Being told you are "not thinking clearly" or "too emotional" to manage things.
- Feeling like a burden for needing space, time, or help.
- Guilt-tripping or manipulation tied to money or inheritance.
- Requests for financial support or access to your assets.
- Being excluded from conversations or decision-making, especially when others begin speaking *about* you rather than *with* you, including with advisors, attorneys, or counselors.

This dynamic is not limited to family, of course. It can also show up in unexpected places. A friendly neighbor. A friend from church. Even the best friend you've had since childhood. People you know, people you love, and people you trust may unintentionally cross boundaries. Some may even begin to rely on your emotional or financial support when you are still trying to stabilize yourself.

If someone begins asking for money, offering "help" that feels pushy or one-sided, or begins influencing your decisions too heavily, pause. You do not have to question their motives, but you *do* have the right (and need) to protect yourself. It's okay to get a second opinion before saying yes. It is okay to say, "I need more time," or "I want to run this by my advisor/attorney/CPA first."

This doesn't mean shutting people out, especially those who care about you and have your best interests at heart. But when emotions are high and decisions carry weight, it can be helpful (and healthy) to have some conversations with professionals one-on-one. A private setting gives you the freedom to ask questions, express concerns, and think clearly without the pressure of someone else's opinion in the room. From there you can return to relationships with more confidence, knowing you've taken the time to think things through on your own terms. Wisdom, especially after a loss, is a form of self-care.

WHEN BOUNDARIES ARE CROSSED

One of my clients, a kind and responsible man in his sixties, came into a modest inheritance after the death of his parents. He used a portion of those funds to do something truly meaningful. He purchased a small home for his adult daughter, who was disabled and living on a fixed income. The inheritance included his parents' longtime home, which he and his wife planned to move into and make their own.

While they were preparing for the transition, he temporarily allowed his adult son to live in the guest house on the property. The son had made some poor choices over the years and was struggling financially. Out of compassion, and the hope that this might help him get back on his feet, our client welcomed him in. But when the time came for our client and his wife to move into the main house, and it was his time to move on, the dynamic shifted. The son became aggressive and demanding. He insisted that he was owed hundreds of thousands of dollars to relocate. The client, shaken and heartbroken, found himself in a painful bind. Fearing for their safety and the care of their home, he and his wife ultimately complied with the son's demands.

What began as generosity was met with coercion, and what should have been a peaceful chapter turned into one marked by fear, betrayal, and silence.

This story is a reminder that boundaries matter, even with the people we love most. Grief, money, and changing family dynamics can bring out complicated emotions in everyone, and not all of them are expressed in healthy ways. If something feels wrong, even with a child or a sibling, it's not betrayal, cruel or selfish to protect yourself. In fact, involving a neutral third party early on, such as an attorney, financial advisor, or even a mediator, can provide the safety and security you need to prevent an uncomfortable situation from spiraling.

YOU STILL GET TO DECIDE

Grief may cloud your thinking, but it doesn't take away your right to make decisions. If something feels off—for example, if you're feeling pushed, controlled, or silenced, it's worth slowing down and speaking with someone outside the family or outside the relationship. A financial advisor, therapist, estate attorney, or even a close friend can help you gain perspective. Sometimes just saying aloud, *"Is this normal?"* is often enough to break the fog.

You are still the decision maker of your life. It's okay to accept help. But it's also okay to say, "Not yet," or "Let me think about that," or "I'd like to talk to my advisor first." That's not disrespect. That's being prudent.

A NEW KIND OF STRENGTH

You did not choose this storm, but you are learning how to stand in it. Even in the midst of grief, even when everything feels unfamiliar, you are making decisions, taking steps, and showing up for your life. That is strength. Not the loud, visible kind that others easily recognize, but the quiet kind that builds a foundation, one thoughtful choice at a time.

CHAPTER TWO

What To Do (and What Not to Do)

The First 30, 60, and 90 Days

The early days of loss are disorienting.
This chapter is here to help steady you.

There's no universal timeline for grief, no checklist that makes this experience easier, and certainly no "right" way to move forward. But there is a practical reality after the death of a spouse, a window of time when certain actions become necessary. Some are time sensitive, while others simply help protect your well-being and lay the groundwork for future decisions.

The first 90 days after losing your spouse are not about reinventing your life. You are not expected to have answers or make sweeping changes. Instead, the goal is to stabilize the most important parts of your financial life, your emotional boundaries, and your ability to move through this process with caution and purpose.

Some days you may feel strong enough to make important decisions. Other days, just opening the mail or returning a phone call may feel like enough. That's okay. The goal here is not speed, it's steadiness. Progress does not need to be dramatic to be meaningful. You are still raw but each step, even the small ones, counts.

The first 90 days after a loss can be broken down into manageable time frames—30 days, 60 days, 90 days—each with specific, realistic goals and gentle guardrails. You'll see what to prioritize, what to delay, and how to protect yourself emotionally and financially along the way. You don't have to do everything listed here, of course, but you may need a place to start.

30 DAYS: STABILIZE AND SECURE

The first 30 days after losing a spouse are often lived in a fog. Emotions come in waves, and routines feel unfamiliar or even meaningless. During this time, your focus should not be on making major life decisions or long-term plans. It should be on stabilizing your life enough to create a foundation you can build from later. Think of this first month as the period where you protect what matters most and begin to sort through the essentials.

Emotionally, you can expect to still be spinning, but there are several critical tasks that must be addressed in these early weeks, even if you feel like you're moving in slow motion. If you haven't already, start by obtaining multiple certified copies of the death certificate. Next, notify key institutions. This includes the Social Security Administration, your spouse's employer or pension provider, and any financial institutions where you hold accounts. If there's life insurance in place, initiate the claims process, but take your time with decisions about what to do with those proceeds. You can park the funds in a savings account or money market fund temporarily.

You'll also need to safeguard the estate. If you and your spouse have shared online accounts or digital records, make sure you can still access them. If you don't know the passwords, you may need help recovering access through the companies involved. These tasks may feel perfunctory and administrative but they are acts of protection, not just of assets but of your peace of mind.

Begin gathering key documents. Don't worry about perfect organization right now, just collect what you can. That includes wills, trust documents, insurance policies, mortgage statements, account summaries, and any bills, especially those in your spouse's name. Don't worry about reviewing the documents, just gather them together in a folder or envelope so that when you are ready to act, you have everything in one place.

During this time it might feel like the best approach is to just keep moving, and certainly that can help distract you from grief. But I strongly encourage you avoid making major decisions right now. For instance, do not feel pressured to sell your home, give away belongings, or make changes to your investment portfolio.

Give yourself permission to move slowly. Stabilizing does not mean solving everything. It means securing what you can, asking for help where needed, and letting the rest wait. This is not procrastination. It is protection, because moving fast does not bypass grief. It only delays it. You cannot outrun heartbreak with efficiency. The pain will wait for you, often resurfacing when you least expect it. Real strength lies in allowing yourself to feel, to pause, and to move through this at a pace that respects both your loss and your healing. In these first 30 days, that is more than enough.

What to Do:

- Secure multiple death certificates (10–15 copies).
- Notify Social Security and employer / pension administrator.
- Begin funeral / memorial planning or follow-up paperwork.
- Locate and protect key documents (wills, insurance, account titles).

- Update or cancel automatic bill payments where appropriate.
- Contact the mortgage company or landlord if necessary.
- Make a list of all known assets and debts.
- Meet with your financial advisor, attorney, or CPA—if you're ready.

What Not to Do:

- Don't feel pressured to make big decisions like selling a home, moving, or changing advisors.
- Don't rush to give away belongings or distribute assets, even to well-meaning family members.
- Don't make any gifts or large financial commitments yet.

Naturally, as the days and weeks pass, your focus needs to shift slightly. Soon, it will no longer be about reacting to your loss but about creating order where there has been chaos. You will need to do more than just notify agencies or collect documents. However, as you approach the end of the first 30 days, you're laying the groundwork for your next important step, which is choosing not to let fear or being overwhelmed drive your life. And that matters.

For most people, the first few weeks after losing a spouse are about stabilization, not resolution. If all you do is gather documents, make a few phone calls, or create space on your calendar to think, consider that great progress. Remember, there is no test to pass or prize for finishing early. What matters most is that you are beginning to turn toward your future, however uncertain it may feel right now.

That said, I've known some clients to take decisive action, even in the early days. One client, after losing his wife following a long and exhausting period of caregiving, quickly put their home on the market, gave away many of their belongings, and set off across the country in an RV. For him, healing began not with stillness, but with movement. He didn't want to pause or process his loss before moving forward. I suspect he's done that along the way, in his own time. However, for most of us, the first 90 days after a loss are often best spent steadying the ship, not dry docking the boat. But of course, that's a guideline, not a rule. Everyone's path is different.

60 DAYS: EVALUATE AND ORGANIZE

By the second month, the immediate whirlwind of paperwork and phone calls have likely started to slow. The shock may still linger, and waves of grief will still come, but there's often just enough space to begin asking, *What now?* This stage is about beginning to regain your footing and gathering your thoughts, your energy, and a sense of direction, however tentative it may feel.

You will probably start to feel the need to better understand your finances. Reviewing your documents, inventorying your assets and liabilities, and getting a handle on your evolving needs may begin to surface as priorities. It still may not be a good idea to finalize big changes yet, so don't feel the need to rush through this. However, by simply gathering the pieces, evaluating what you have, and organizing your world, it will begin to feel a little less uncertain.

Start by taking a closer look at your income sources. Make a list of what is still coming in and what might be changing. This could include:

- **Social Security survivor benefits**—which may be based on your spouse's work record or your own
- **pension payments**, if applicable
- **investment income** such as dividends, interest, or automatic withdrawals
- **annuities**, rental income, or other structured payments

If you haven't already, contact the Social Security Administration and, if applicable, your spouse's former employer to confirm what benefits you're entitled to and whether any paperwork is outstanding. This step alone can offer relief by identifying exactly what income you can depend upon on a regular basis.

Once you know what's coming in, it is time to begin to map out a basic cash flow plan. You don't need a complicated budget, just a simple overview of what money is arriving each month and what is going out. Of course, it may be helpful to do this with your financial advisor if you have one. They may have a budget worksheet that can help ensure you don't miss anything important or can enable you to focus on the essentials. You will want to account for housing, utilities, insurance, groceries, and medical needs. If there are unnecessary expenses or automatic drafts you no longer use or need, cancel them.

This is also the right time to confirm account access and review how your accounts are titled. Are your bank and investment accounts now in your name? Do you have online access to everything you'll need moving forward? Have you updated the beneficiary information on your IRAs and retirement plans? Take your time, but be sure each account reflects your current legal status. This helps avoid confusion or delays down the road. It also ensures that your advisors can legally assist you as needed. Keep in mind that most accounts, especially investment or brokerage accounts, are frozen upon death. No money can be moved, no trades can be placed, and no changes can be made under the deceased spouse's Social Security number, even when held in joint accounts. Consequently, retitling the account is often a necessary first step to regaining access and control.

In this phase, it's wise to begin thinking about your own estate planning documents, even if you're not ready to make all the big decisions just yet. This includes:

- Durable Power of Attorney—someone who can make financial decisions on your behalf if needed
- Health Care Directive or Advance Medical Directive—in case of future medical events.
- Will or Trust—revised and reflecting your current intentions and circumstances.

If you have not yet met with your own estate attorney or need to find one who better understands your needs, this is a good time to begin that conversation. Again, you need not worry about finalizing everything now, but you should ensure that nothing is outdated, invalid, or potentially problematic if something unexpected happens to you.

If you are emotionally ready, it's recommended that you use this period to meet with professionals or start reaching out to find ones if you don't have them already. Whether it's your financial advisor, CPA, or attorney, these individuals can help you see what you might have missed, offer reassurance, and begin to guide your longer-term planning. If you've been working with your spouse's advisors and it doesn't feel like a good fit, or if you feel like a passive participant, it's okay to begin interviewing new professionals who speak to *your* goals, not just your spouse's legacy.

In the resources section you will find a link to a guide for finding a financial advisor.

Lastly, review your insurance coverage. This includes:

- health insurance—make sure you're still covered under the right policy or Medicare plan
- life insurance—determine if any policies are still active, and whether new coverage is needed
- homeowners and auto insurance—make sure the policies reflect correct ownership

- long-term care insurance, if applicable—understand what it covers and how to access it if ever needed

What Not to Do in This Stage

It may feel like it's time to "do something." You may want to feel in control and just need to take action to feel alive. This might be with your investments, your home, or your family plans, but in most cases, this is not the time for major financial moves. Unless absolutely necessary, it's best to avoid making major financial decisions including large investments or reallocations in your portfolio. Markets may be volatile, but your emotions are probably still quite raw. This is, ideally, a time to observe and organize, not overhaul.

- Don't finalize investment reallocations unless you've reviewed them carefully, ideally with a fiduciary advisor.
- Don't sign any contracts, financial agreements, or legal documents you don't fully understand. Always ask for time and review them with someone you trust.
- Don't let guilt, fear, or pressure from family or anyone else drive your decisions, especially around financial support or shared property.

This stage really should be about gaining clarity, not certainty. You do not have to feel in control of everything, and you certainly don't have to have it all figured out. Grief is still present, and your life may still feel foreign. That's normal. However, the steps you are taking now, reviewing your income, confirming account access, organizing key documents, are very meaningful. These aren't just administrative tasks. They are signs that you are beginning to reclaim your space, your voice, and your future. If you are finding this step difficult, give yourself credit for the little things that you are doing. And no matter what, give yourself time and space to consider the larger things.

You are not expected to solve everything at once. In fact, trying to do so would likely leave you feeling even more overwhelmed. What matters now is that you are beginning to see the landscape more clearly. You're asking questions, gathering facts, and giving yourself the ability to think before acting. That is progress, and what healing looks like at this point.

Each phone call made, each file sorted, each document reviewed all add up. You are moving forward, even if it doesn't always feel like it. And you're doing it on your terms, at your pace. That's not just something to be proud of, it's something that will serve you well in every step ahead.

90 DAYS: BEGIN TO RECLAIM

By the 90-day mark, life will likely still feel unfamiliar. Your grief hasn't disappeared, and your routines surely still feel unsettled, but there is often a subtle shift where you are no longer living entirely in response to what has happened. You are beginning to move forward, even if only a little. This is the stage where intention starts to take the place of reaction. It is about taking your first steps into the new person you are now. You are someone who has endured great loss, but who still has a life to live.

You may find yourself thinking differently about your future. You may be asking new questions: *What do I want my life to look like now? What do I need to feel secure? Who do I trust to help me get there?* The answers don't need to be immediate or final, but allowing yourself to ask those questions is, in itself, a sign of healing.

Financially, this is the time to start to build or revise your retirement income plan. Your life has changed in significant ways, and your financial plan needs to reflect that. What once worked for you as part of a couple may no longer apply. Now, your financial plan needs to be designed around your needs, your goals, and your comfort level as a single person.

This may involve re-evaluating several key areas:

- Your Social Security strategy, especially if survivor benefits are available.
- Any pension benefits reduced or lost or any annuity options you now hold independently.
- Your withdrawal plan from retirement accounts, which may need to be adjusted for RMDs, tax efficiency and longevity.
- Your investment allocation, which may no longer match your current risk tolerance or time horizon.

Even your day-to-day financial rhythm may look different now, so your income needs may change. You may be spending more money in some areas and less in others. Your cash flow needs may need to be adjusted within your planning assumptions, and your long-term priorities, such as staying in your home, traveling, or preserving assets for heirs, may need to be reconsidered through a new lens.

Most of all, this is a time to create a comprehensive plan that helps you feel secure, supported, and in control. The plan you had before was built around a different life, one shaped by shared goals or someone else's vision for the future. Now you need a plan that reflects where you are today and can evolve with you as your life continues to change.

If you've been working with an advisor, this is the time to determine whether you feel truly supported or whether it's time to establish new professional relationships. The same goes for your CPA or attorney. You are now the decision-maker, and you deserve a team that recognizes your voice and respects your pace.

This may also be a good time to review and start to work on revising your estate plan, if you haven't already. Your family structure, financial circumstances, and long-term goals have changed, and your legal documents should reflect that. Update your will or trust. Revisit your powers of attorney and health care directives. Think about who you want to name in those roles, and whether any changes are needed based on your current reality.

On the emotional side, this is also a good time to consider joining a support group or widow's community, if you haven't already. Many people wait until they feel more emotionally "put together" to seek support, but that's often backwards. Support is what helps you rebuild. It's not the reward for already having done so. Whether it's a grief group, a spiritual community, or simply a new friendship that feels nourishing, these connections can offer strength in ways you may not expect.

What Not to Do

As you begin to reclaim your future, remember that not all advice is helpful. Well-meaning friends or relatives may encourage you to "move on," "clean house," or "start fresh," but your timeline is your own. You are not obligated to rush anything just to make others feel comfortable.

- Don't make major life changes to appease others.
- Don't compare your progress or grief to anyone else's.
- Don't assume that by now, you should "have it all figured out." You are still building, still healing.

Ninety days certainly does not mark the end of your grief, but it can mark the beginning of your authority. There's a common saying that marriage is "two people becoming one," as if each person was incomplete, but marriage is not two halves becoming a whole. It's two whole people walking side by side. You were a whole person before, and you are still a whole person now, even if you don't feel like it.

Naturally, you don't feel the same today as you did when you had the security of your spouse. You are not the same. But you are still wise. Still capable. Still *here.* And from this place, you can begin to shape what comes next, defined by what you choose to build.

If you are struggling with confidence, that's normal. It's one decision at a time, one brave moment at a time. Your future still matters so, ideally, you are moving from the question, *What now?* toward *What's next?*—not in haste, but in courage. You've already made it through the hardest part. Now, step forward because this is where your life continues, and moving with intention, grace, and the strength to choose what comes next will shape your tomorrow.

CHAPTER THREE

Your Home

Should You Stay or Should You Go?

Grief may shape you, but it does not define you.
What you do next—that's you.

There's no roadmap for the choices you're facing now. Some days it feels like everything in your life is up for reevaluation, from the house you're living in to the people you let into your space to the accounts and investments you own. Widowhood has a way of placing you at a crossroads, over and over again. And with every crossroads comes a question: *Do I hold on to this or let it go?* These aren't easy decisions, and they're rarely black and white, but what I've learned, both personally and through the widows and widowers I've walked beside, is that your ability to navigate these decisions efficiently will shape not just your finances, but your future peace of mind.

This isn't just about dollars and cents. It's about ownership. Ownership is deeper than a title on a deed or a name on an account. It's about owning your life, your time, your energy, and what comes next. Knowing whether you should stay in your home or go isn't just an investment strategy, it's a life strategy. And like all good strategies, it requires reflection, courage, and a willingness to be honest with yourself about what no longer fits.

THE HOUSE THAT HOLDS YOUR HEART

One of the most emotionally charged decisions you may face is what to do with your home. It's not just where you live, it's where your memories live. Every corner might hold a moment. The chair he always sat in, the kitchen where she made coffee every morning, the patio where you had family barbecues, the dining table where you talked about growing old together. And now you're left with the question: Should I stay? Or is it time to go?

This is extremely personal. There's no right answer, and anyone who tries to tell you otherwise hasn't walked in your shoes. For some, staying put offers comfort and continuity. It's familiar, it's grounding, and it provides a sense of safety when everything else feels like it's collapsed. But for others, the house becomes too quiet, too large, or too heavy. The upkeep becomes a burden or the silence is deafening. Sometimes, holding onto the house feels more like holding onto the past, and that's not always healing.

LETTING GO OR HOLDING ON

Letting go is not just about relocating. It's what happens in your heart. It's the emotional permission to release something. Relocating is the next step. It's when you act on that permission and choose what's next. You don't owe anyone that choice but yourself.

Are you comfortable in your current home? Is it manageable physically, financially, and emotionally? Would downsizing make sense, or do you want to stay where you are for now?

Relocating is a major decision. It is one that should be made thoughtfully. You may not be prepared to make any decisions at this time, but it's okay to begin imagining what "home" looks like for you in this new life.

Deciding whether to stay or go is never just a financial choice. It is emotional. Staying in your home because it still gives you comfort is one thing. Choosing to leave, or starting fresh somewhere else, is where letting go comes in. Understanding the difference gives you permission to move at your own pace without pressure.

One of our longtime clients, we'll call him George, lost his wife of 50 years. They had lived in the same house for more than three decades. It was a home filled with memories, photos, and the echoes of children growing up. His grandchildren, who had spent countless holidays there, begged him to keep the house. *Grandpa, you can't sell it,* they said. *It's home.*

At the time, George agreed. He told me in no uncertain terms that he had no plans to move. It was where he and his wife had built their life together. It was familiar. It was comforting. Letting go of it felt unthinkable.

But grief changes. And so does life.

After five years alone in the house, George reluctantly admitted the neighborhood wasn't the same anymore. Most of his longtime neighbors had moved away. He didn't know the families around him. The sounds that used to fill the home, his wife in the kitchen, the grandkids running down the hall, had been replaced by silence. "I'm just lonely," he said to me.

He had started spending time with friends who lived in a retirement community just a few miles away. They were active, connected, and engaged. While he watched from a distance, they were hosting dinners, going to events, playing pickleball during the day and poker in the evenings. George began to see hope for a different kind of life. He wanted one where support and companionship were part of his daily rhythm. So, eventually, he made the decision to move. It was not because the house meant any less to him, but because he realized he wanted something more for himself. He knew that was something his wife would have wanted, too. George deserved community, connection, and the kind of support to help him thrive, not just get by.

Not everyone will relate to George's journey, and that's okay. Some people know right away that they want or need to move. Others may remain in the same home for the rest of their lives and feel perfectly content there. And some, like George, won't know until years have passed that their needs have changed.

The important thing is not to force a decision before you're ready. But it's also important to allow yourself room to consider your options. Don't avoid thinking about alternatives simply out of guilt or pressure from others. What worked when you were a couple may not serve you as a single person. A home can hold memories and comfort, but it can also involve isolation or unnecessary responsibility. Only you can know which.

Downsizing doesn't mean loss. Sometimes it means choosing something that fits your life as it is now, not as it once was. I'm reminded of another client; we'll call them Linda and Scott. They moved to Arizona when Scott retired. It had been their dream for years—sunshine, golf, open skies. They packed up their life in California and relocated with excitement for their next chapter. But just two weeks after their move, Scott died suddenly of a heart attack. He was only 67 years old.

When Linda called to tell me the news, I could hear the shock and sadness in her voice, but also a resolve. She told me she had already called her agent to put the house up for sale. "Arizona was *our* dream," Linda said. "It wasn't my dream." She moved back to California, to a smaller home near the neighborhood she had lived in for over 20 years. It wasn't what she had pictured for her retirement, but it felt familiar. It felt like home. And for her, that made all the difference.

Of course, if you're not ready to make that decision yet, and I would argue that such a decision is far too big to make while still in shock, that's perfectly fine. There is no rush. You'll know when, or if, the time is right.

In the case of Linda, I understood completely. She hadn't even finished unpacking. Her husband was gone, and suddenly she was alone in an unfamiliar place, surrounded by boxes and silence. The thought of starting over and making new friends, finding new doctors, and navigating new streets felt daunting. So she chose what felt familiar. She went back to where she had roots and where she felt known. For her, that was the right decision.

Let your choice be guided by what supports your well-being, not by guilt, not by sentiment, and not by what others think you should do. Whether you stay in your home, move near to your children, or start fresh somewhere new, the goal is to live in a space that offers you peace, connection, and the freedom to shape a future that feels right for you on your terms, in your time.

If you're feeling like it may be time to go, but you also feel guilty, remember selling doesn't mean erasing your life together. It doesn't mean leaving him or her behind. It means you are choosing what works for you now. It means freeing up resources, simplifying responsibilities, and giving yourself the space to imagine what comes next. And yes, it might mean crying in the driveway one last time, but it's also opening the door to something new. Something lighter. Something that reflects the new person you are today.

Of course, if you're wrestling with this, don't rush to make a decision. Give yourself permission to sit with the choice. Talk it out. Run the numbers. Picture your life both ways—staying and going—and pay attention to what feels like peace, not just what feels familiar. The house is just a structure. Home is the life you create within it.

My Own Experience: Letting Go and Moving Forward

Years ago I went through a divorce that, like most, marked the end of a life I once thought I had set. My former husband and I had built what we called our "dream home." We were there when the foundation was poured and made every decision together, down to the placement of every electrical outlet and the color of every cabinet. It was thrilling to watch our home come to life, but as the marriage unraveled, the beauty of the house, the custom details and the memories all began to feel like ties that kept me there for the wrong reason.

Letting go of that house was difficult. But I'll never forget the moment after the boxes were packed and all that remained were dust bunnies in the corners and empty nail holes where our pictures had once hung, when I stood in that quiet space and realized it was just a structure. Wood, stone, and concrete. It no longer felt like home. And as I drove away for the last time, it was strangely freeing. The farther I got from the street, the clearer the sky seemed, and I began to feel something I hadn't in a long time—forward-looking.

Now, I share this not to compare divorce to death, because those are profoundly different kinds of grief. But what I learned is that sometimes letting go of a home is part of letting go a life as it once was. And in widowhood that may also be true. If something smaller, simpler, or more "you" feels like it would give you breathing room, don't dismiss that instinct. A new space, whether it's a different house or simply a fresh start, can be part of your healing.

That said, if your home brings you comfort, if the history wrapped within its walls soothes your spirit, then let it continue to hold you. Let it be a place where healing can happen gently, surrounded by what's familiar. The decision isn't about right or wrong. It's about what helps you feel whole again.

The Financial Side of Staying or Selling

Beyond the emotional weight of staying or leaving, there is the financial cost and it's not insignificant. A house that once made perfect sense for two people may now feel oversized, in terms of both in space and expense. Maintenance, property taxes, utilities, landscaping, and unexpected repairs add up. And if your income has been cut, or you're drawing from savings now instead of building more, those costs can start to feel less like comfort and more like pressure.

You might be retired, but the house isn't. It still needs tending to. Roofs wear out, water heaters break, and yards don't mow themselves. If you're paying for help because you no longer want or are able to manage it all on your own, that is another layer of expense. Even if the mortgage is gone, the costs of staying put can slowly but surely eat into your financial security.

And then there's opportunity cost. Maybe the equity in your home could be doing more for you elsewhere, like supporting your retirement income, allowing you to travel, helping with future care needs, or simply buying you peace of mind. Sometimes downsizing isn't just about space. It's about cash flow and reclaiming flexibility.

These aren't easy decisions, of course. But it's worth asking yourself: Am I living in a home that supports the life I want now? Or am I holding onto a house that fits who I used to be?

There's no shame in saying *this is too much*. That's not giving up. That's being wise. As I learned when I sold my dream house, home is a feeling, not a square footage or an address. If finances are tight and your house has become a burden, it's okay to reimagine what *home* could look like. Smaller can be freer. Less can be more. And letting go can sometimes be the most financially and emotionally responsible choice you can make.

When the House Costs More Than It Gives

Let's talk about the numbers. Sometimes seeing the math is what finally helps things click. If your current home is paid off but costs $12,000 per year in property taxes, insurance, and maintenance, that's $1,000 a month before you even turn on a light switch. Add utilities, landscaping, and the occasional repair or appliance replacement, and you could be spending $1,500 to $2,000 a month just to live in a home that may no longer serve you.

Now, imagine you sell that home and purchase a smaller one or a condo or townhouse. Not only could you free up equity that can be invested or used to supplement your income, but your ongoing costs may also drop. For instance, your property taxes could fall, and so too could your maintenance costs. If you have homeowners association (HOA) dues, they will likely include landscaping, exterior maintenance, and possibly even some utilities. In short, downsizing could reduce your annual housing expenses, which could then be used to finance travel, help ensure you don't run out of savings, or build a cushion to give you greater financial security.

Downsizing might also reduce your need to pull as much from retirement accounts, especially taxable ones. That could help keep your tax bracket lower and avoid costly Medicare surcharges. In other words, a smaller home doesn't just feel lighter, *it is* often lighter across the board.

Let's say you're still carrying a mortgage that costs $2,200 a month with 10 years remaining, and now you're on a tighter fixed income. Without your spouse's income, or with lower Social Security benefits or a reduced pension, that monthly obligation can start to feel more like a weight than a shelter. Downsizing into a mortgage-free property or moving into a 55+ community with streamlined ownership costs might not just lower your expenses, it could also ease the financial anxiety that comes with trying to stretch limited income to cover rising costs. In this case, it could represent over a quarter of a million dollars.

Many people overlook this point. The earlier you make that move, the more time your capital has to work for you. Compound interest works best not just with time, but with larger principal amounts. Holding onto a high-cost home for too long, especially if you're dipping into savings to keep up, can erode the base you need for your money to grow. Selling earlier, freeing up equity, and investing those funds can potentially preserve capital and may generate more income over time. Don't wait until you're forced to make a move under financial pressure. Proactive choices help you stay in control, sustain savings for longer, and reduce the risk of depletion later on when you may have fewer options.

It's not just about financial gain, of course. It is also about comfort and convenience. Downsizing might mean a newer home with efficient appliances, modern safety features, or no stairs, each of which could save you from costly home modifications down the road. Proximity to shops, community centers, or medical services can also reduce your reliance on driving or paid help.

The point here isn't to compel you to sell, but to show that your options may deserve a second look. Downsizing isn't a downgrade. In many cases, it's a strategic, empowering move that can reduce risk, improve cash flow, and open up more of what you actually want in the life ahead.

Clarity through Planning, Not Pressure

Naturally, before you put a For Sale sign in the yard, it's important to understand how selling your home could impact your taxes. This is especially true if your house has appreciated significantly in value over the years. The good news is that, in many cases, you may not owe any capital gains taxes at all. But there are a few key rules to know.

As a single person, you can exclude up to $250,000 of capital gains from the sale of your primary residence, as long as you've owned and lived in the home for at least two of the last five years. Married couples, however, can exclude up to $500,000. Now this is important because you have a two-year window now where you may be able to sell your home and still use the $500,000 exclusion. Of course, this is provided you haven't remarried and you meet the other ownership and use tests which I'll describe later. But after that two-year period, the IRS treats you as a single seller so only the $250,000 exclusion applies.

Let me give you an example. Let's say you and your spouse bought your home for $300,000 and it's now worth $750,000. If you sell it for that amount, your gain is $450,000. As a widow, you can exclude $250,000 of gain from income taxes. That means the remaining $200,000 would be subject to capital gains tax which, depending on your income, might be taxed at 15 or 20 percent, plus possibly a 3.8 percent net investment income tax. That's potentially $30,000 to $47,600 in tax liability as a result of selling your home.

But if you qualify for the surviving spouse rule under Section 121, you could use the full $500,000 gain exclusion. That is, if you sell your home within two years of your spouse's death. So, in this example, you could receive the full $450,000 income tax free, saving you a lot of money. To qualify, though, you must meet the same ownership and use tests that apply to all home sellers. You must have owned the home and used it as your primary residence for at least two of the five years before the sale, and you cannot have remarried before the sale. These rules, along with other details in IRS Publication 523, should be reviewed with your tax or financial advisor. But this break could shield you from paying taxes, possibly on the entire gain. However, timing is critical. Once the two-year window closes, the exclusion drops back to $250,000.

Also, make sure your cost basis is adjusted correctly. Cost basis is defined as the original purchase price of your home plus the cost of any capital improvements you've made over time. Getting this number right is essential, because it determines how much of your sale proceeds count as taxable gain after applying the home sale exclusion. Let's say you bought your home for $400,000. But over the years, you added a new roof for $25,000 and remodeled the kitchen for $50,000. Your adjusted cost basis would then be $400,000 plus the $75,000 you spent on improvements, or $475,000. If you sold the house for $650,000, your gain would be $175,000 ($650,000 minus $475,000) which may be fully excluded from tax under the home sale exclusion rules if you meet the ownership and use requirements.

Now, if your home was jointly owned and you live in a community property state like California, your cost basis may be "stepped up" to the fair market value at your spouse's date of death for the *entire property*. In non-community property states, only half of the property gets the step-up. That step-up can significantly reduce or even eliminate capital gains taxes, but it has to be properly documented, usually with an appraisal and sound recordkeeping. More on that later.

Clearly, before you decide to sell, it's worth having your tax or financial advisor run the numbers and clarify:

- What's your adjusted cost basis (purchase price plus improvements)?
- Do you qualify for the $250,000 or $500,000 exclusion?
- Do you qualify for a step up in basis?
- Is it financially better to sell now or wait?

This isn't just a tax issue, however. You don't want the tax savings to press you to do something you aren't ready or wanting to do. But since this is a life decision that could have lasting financial consequences, understanding the tax rules helps you make decisions that are both emotionally and financially sound.

UNDERSTANDING CAPITAL GAINS, STEP-UP IN BASIS, AND TRUST OWNERSHIP WHEN SELLING YOUR HOME

It's important to understand how taxes may affect the sale of your property, even if you aren't selling at this time. This is one area where timing, titling, and state laws all intersect, and getting the details right can make a significant difference in how much of your equity you get to keep.

First, let's start with the federal capital gains exclusion. As already mentioned, if you sell your primary residence, the IRS allows you to exclude up to $250,000 of gain from taxation as a single filer. If you are married and filing jointly at the time of sale, the exclusion doubles to $500,000. Remember, if you are widowed, you may still be able to use the full $500,000 exclusion if you sell the home within two years of your spouse's death, provided the home qualified as your primary residence for at least two out of the last five years and you otherwise met the married filing joint requirements before your spouse's death. If, on the other hand, more than two years have passed, then you're generally limited to the $250,000 single filer exclusion.

(If you remarry, you may again qualify for the full $500,000 home sale exclusion, but only if you and your new spouse meet the Section 121 ownership and residency requirements, file a joint return, and neither of you has claimed a home sale exclusion within the prior two years).

Nevertheless, the exclusion is only one piece of the tax puzzle. Equally important is understanding your cost basis, which determines how much of the sale price is considered a gain. This is where the step-up in basis comes into play. When one spouse dies, the IRS allows the cost basis of certain assets, such as a home, stocks, or other non-retirement investments, to be "stepped up" to their fair market value as of the date of death. This step-up can significantly reduce, or even eliminate, capital gains taxes when the asset is later sold. And unlike the capital gains exclusion, which may expire after two years or become unavailable if your circumstances change, the step-up in basis is permanent. It's a quiet, often overlooked benefit, but one that can offer lasting financial protection if understood and used wisely.

Now, what that step-up looks like, as noted, depends on what state you live in and how the property was owned. In community property states (California, Arizona, Texas, Idaho, Louisiana, Nevada, New Mexico, Washington and Wisconsin), if the home was considered community property, the entire property generally receives a full step-up in basis. This applies not just to the deceased spouse's half, but to the entire property, which receives a full step-up in basis to its fair market value as of the date of death. Therefore, if you and your spouse bought your home for $300,000, and it was worth $700,000 when your spouse passed, your adjusted cost basis may become $700,000. That means if you subsequently sell it for that amount, there would be no capital gain to tax. The home sale gain exclusion wouldn't even be needed.

On the other hand, if you live in a common law state (that is, any state not listed as a community property state, except for Alaska, which allows couples to elect community property treatment through a formal community property agreement), only your spouse's half of the home typically receives a step-up in basis upon their death. Your half retains its original cost basis.

Let's break that down with the same example: Suppose you and your spouse bought your home years ago for $300,000. Under common law rules, when a home is jointly owned, each spouse is generally presumed to own 50 percent of the property, so each of you has a cost basis of $150,000. Now let's say your spouse passes away and the home is worth $700,000 at the time of his/her death. Only their half receives a step-up to fair market value, so their basis increases from $150,000 to $350,000 (half of the date of death market value). Your half, however, remains at its original basis of $150,000. That gives you a combined new stepped-up cost basis of $500,000 ($350,000 plus $150,000).

If you subsequently sell the home for $700,000, the capital gain would be $200,000 ($700,000 sale price minus $500,000 adjusted basis). Fortunately, as a single filer, you may qualify for the $250,000 home sale exclusion (under IRS Section 121), which would fully offset the gain in this example, meaning no capital gains tax would be due. However, if the appreciation was higher or the home sold for more, a portion of the gain could become taxable.

Finally, it's important to understand what cost basis on your home actually means. Remember, your cost basis is essentially the amount of money you've invested in your home, and although it typically starts with your original purchase price, it doesn't stop there. Cost basis also includes certain closing costs (like title insurance or legal fees) and capital improvements you've made over the years such as a kitchen remodel, roof replacement, room addition, or solar installation. Routine maintenance and repairs don't count, but upgrades that add value or extend the life of the home do. If you've owned the house a long time, your cost basis may be quite different than your original purchase price. Therefore, keeping good records of all improvements and knowing your basis is key to calculating the taxable gain when you eventually sell the home.

HOMES TITLED IN A LIVING TRUST

Do living trusts complicate things? Not usually. If your home is titled in a revocable living trust, which is common for estate planning purposes, you can still receive the same step-up in basis as long as the trust was properly structured and both spouses were grantors (the people who created and funded the trust) and beneficiaries (the people who benefit from the trust while living). The IRS treats a properly structured revocable trust as an extension of the individual for tax purposes, meaning the home is still considered personally owned. As a result, the step-up in basis still applies. In community property states, however, the trust needs to clearly identify the property as community property in order for the entire home to qualify for a full step-up (not just the deceased spouse's share). The key is how the trust is written and titled, which is why having it reviewed by an estate attorney is so important.

Where you can run into trouble is if the trust was *irrevocable* before your spouse's death, or if the home was titled in a way that doesn't clearly show it as community property. In those cases, only part, or perhaps none of the home may get a step-up. Similarly, if the trust separates assets into individual "his" and "hers" buckets (commonly known as "A/B Trusts") without classifying the home as community property, it may unintentionally reduce the step-up opportunity.

This is one of the many reasons why it's so important to review your trust and titling with a qualified estate attorney. In Chapter Seven, I write about estate planning and trusts. Small paperwork decisions made years ago can have major tax implications when you're ready to sell.

In short, don't confuse the home capital gains exclusion with the step-up in basis. These are two separate benefits that work together. The exclusion helps protect the gain, while the step-up helps minimize how much gain is calculated in the first place. And with proper planning, especially in community property states, it's possible to dramatically reduce or even eliminate capital gains taxes on the sale of a home. Knowing how the rules apply to your situation can give you greater financial flexibility, and more importantly, peace of mind when deciding whether to stay or go.

How to Document a Step-Up in Basis after the Death of a Spouse

Regardless of whether you chose to stay or go, the step-up in basis is not automatic. You need to document it properly. The time to do that is upon death, even if you don't plan to sell for years. Consequently, one of the most important steps to take right now is to have the property professionally appraised as of the date of your spouse's death and to keep that documentation permanently in your records. This establishes your stepped-up basis and can save you a significant amount in capital gains tax if and when you eventually sell.

The most straightforward way to document a step-up in basis is to hire a licensed real estate appraiser to determine the fair market value of your home as of the date of your spouse's death. Keep the full appraisal report in your records along with a copy of the death certificate. If you have more than one property, repeat the process for each one.

If it has been a year or more, you can still obtain a retrospective appraisal, which is an appraisal performed now but based on market data from the date of death. This often requires the appraiser to research historical sales and comparable properties from that period. While a retrospective appraisal can cost more and take longer, it can still establish the stepped-up basis you are entitled to. The key is to have credible, third-party documentation. Without it, the IRS could challenge your numbers years later, and you might end up paying more in taxes than necessary.

As already highlighted, the step-up in cost basis can dramatically reduce the taxable gain if and when you eventually sell and, should you have to prove what the home was worth at the time of death, an appraisal on file can protect you down the road. Without it, you may be stuck scrambling for old records or worse, end up paying taxes on gains that never should have been taxable in the first place.

CHANGING TITLE ON PROPERTY

For many couples, their home is titled jointly, either as joint tenants with right of survivorship or held in a shared living trust. These arrangements are designed to ease the transition when one spouse passes away, but that transition is not entirely automatic. Legal ownership must still be formally recorded. If your home was held in joint tenancy with rights of survivorship, you are now the sole legal owner, but the deed must be updated to reflect that. This typically involves filing an affidavit of death along with a certified copy of the death certificate with the county recorder. Until that's done, your late spouse's name remains on title, which can complicate future sales, refinancing, or estate administration.

If the home was held in a joint living trust, the process may be slightly different but equally important. While the trust likely includes instructions for what happens after one spouse dies, you may need to work with your estate attorney to formally administer the trust and transfer title to a survivor's trust or individual trust, depending on the structure. Ignoring this step could lead to delays, confusion, or unintended tax consequences down the line.

It may seem like a minor technicality during an already overwhelming time, but updating property title is one of those essential steps that protects your rights, simplifies future decisions, and honors the legal process set in motion when your spouse passed. Step into your new role with control and order, and if you're unsure where to start, reach out to your estate attorney or financial advisor. This isn't something you have to figure out alone, but it is something that should be done.

WHAT ABOUT MORTGAGE DEBT?

If the mortgage was held in both your names, you are generally still responsible for the remaining payments after your spouse's death. Most mortgages are structured so that the obligation continues with the surviving borrower, without any need to refinance or requalify. You simply continue making payments as usual. However, it's important to notify the lender of your spouse's passing and ensure that their records are updated appropriately. If the mortgage was only in your spouse's name, but you jointly owned the home, you still have legal rights to the property, and federal protections such as the Garn-St. Germain Act often prevent lenders from calling the loan due solely because of death. In some cases, refinancing the loan may be appropriate, depending on your long-term plans and the lender's requirements. Either way, reviewing the mortgage terms and title structure with your advisor or estate attorney ensures you're protected and that no surprises emerge later in the process.

In addition to getting the appraisal and changing the title, you'll want to retain a certified copy of the death certificate, as well as documents that show how the property was titled for future IRS purposes. It matters whether the home was held as community property, joint tenancy, or in a revocable trust, as already highlighted. If you live in a community property state, and the home was clearly owned as community property, the entire home may receive a step-up in basis and proving that with proper documentation can be worth tens of thousands, or even hundreds of thousands of dollars in tax savings. In common law states, typically only the deceased spouse's half receives a step-up, while your half retains its original basis, but that also needs to be substantiated if ever challenged. The difference can be significant, especially for homes that have appreciated substantially over time.

If your home was held in a revocable living trust, don't worry. The step-up still applies as long as the trust was structured properly and the home was characterized correctly for tax purposes. But the trust documents should clearly indicate ownership and, if applicable, community property status. It's a good idea to have your estate attorney review the trust to confirm everything is in order.

If a full appraisal wasn't done at the time of death, you might still be able to obtain a retrospective appraisal, which is an appraisal prepared today, based on the home's estimated value as of the date of death. This is a common approach in estate situations, especially when no sale occurred at the time. You can also use comparable sales from that period to help support your valuation, though this method is generally considered less reliable and may be more susceptible to IRS scrutiny. While a retrospective appraisal is accepted by the IRS when done properly, it's important to work with a qualified real estate appraiser who understands the requirements for tax reporting. If challenged, having clear documentation and professional support can go a long way in defending your valuation.

Finally, even if no estate tax return (Form 706) is required because the estate falls under the exemption threshold, you should know that it's still your responsibility to maintain clear records of the step-up for future reference. The key is to keep all documents, especially the appraisal, deed, death certificate, and trust papers together in your estate file.

This might sound like a lot, especially in the midst of grief, but taking the time to gather and store this documentation is one of the most practical, protective financial steps you can take. The step-up in basis is a valuable tool, but only if you can prove it when it matters.

QUESTIONS TO ASK YOUR ESTATE ATTORNEY

These questions will help ensure your trust, property title, and legal documents are aligned with your current situation and financial goals:

1. Is my home titled correctly in the trust, and does the trust clearly show how the property was owned—jointly, individually, or as community property?
2. Does the trust documentation preserve the step-up in basis now that my spouse has passed?
3. Am I fully protected as the surviving spouse, and is there anything I need to do now that my spouse is gone?
4. Are there steps I should take to retitle the property, remove my spouse's name, or prepare for future inheritance?
5. Do I need to update or restate my trust based on my spouse's death or a recent move to a new state?

6. Is the home eligible for a full step-up in basis under my state's property laws?
7. If my home is in a trust, is it still considered part of my estate for tax purposes?
8. What other legal documents should I review or update now—such as my power of attorney, health care directive, or successor trustee designation?

QUESTIONS TO ASK YOUR CPA OR FINANCIAL ADVISOR

These questions will help you understand the tax consequences of selling your home after your spouse's death, and how to document everything correctly:

1. What is my new cost basis in the home after my spouse's passing?
2. Should I get a date-of-death appraisal to document the fair market value of the home?
3. Do I qualify for the $500,000 capital gains exclusion, and is there a deadline to sell in order to use it?
4. How will my state's laws affect the step-up in basis or capital gains calculation?
5. How should I document capital improvements I've made to the home to support a higher cost basis?
6. If my home is in a revocable living trust, how does that impact the capital gains reporting when I sell?

Will Selling the Home Affect My Taxes, Medicare Irmaa, or Other Income-Based Thresholds?

Before you sell your home, it's important to understand how the proceeds, or more specifically the taxable gain, could affect other areas of your financial life. Even if you don't owe capital gains tax because of the home sale exclusion, the reported gain still shows up on your tax return. And that can ripple into other areas, including your Medicare premiums. Medicare uses something called IRMAA (Income-Related Monthly Adjustment Amount) to determine whether you'll pay higher premiums for Parts B and D. The thresholds are based on your Modified Adjusted Gross Income (MAGI) from two years prior. (You can read all about it in Chapter Six).

Suffice it to say, a large gain in the year you sell, even if you don't owe tax on it, can push your income above those IRMAA limits and cause your Medicare premiums to spike temporarily, if you sell at age 63 or later. In addition, a higher adjusted gross income might also reduce your eligibility for certain tax deductions, increase how much of your Social Security benefit is taxed, or bump you into a higher marginal bracket for other income. That's why it's wise to have your CPA or advisor run a projection before you sell—not just to calculate the gain, but to estimate the impact across your broader financial picture. Even a well-planned home sale can create unintended consequences if you're not looking at the whole landscape.

To put this into perspective, let's look at a real-world example. Susan, a 68-year-old widow, decided to sell the home she and her husband had lived in for 30 years. They had purchased it decades ago for $250,000, and she sold it for $850,000 after his passing. Thanks to the step-up in basis and the $250,000 home sale exclusion available to her as a single filer, Susan didn't owe any capital gains tax because the adjusted basis after her husband's death brought the gain down significantly.

However, the IRS still required her to report the capital gain—about $200,000 after all calculations—as part of her Adjusted Gross Income (AGI). That one-year spike in income pushed her Modified Adjusted Gross Income (MAGI) above the Medicare

IRMAA threshold. Two years later, and much to her surprise, her Part B premium increased by nearly $5,000 for the year, and her Part D prescription drug premium also rose. She wasn't penalized or taxed on the home sale itself, but the additional "phantom income" on paper triggered temporary surcharges in her Medicare costs.

When her income returned to normal levels, her Medicare premiums were automatically adjusted back down in subsequent years. Still, it was an unexpected expense she wished she had known about earlier. A quick consultation with her CPA or financial advisor before the sale could have prepared her for the ripple effect or possibly helped her time the sale differently to avoid or minimize the impact.

If you've already sold your home or are concerned about IRMAA adjustments after a one-time spike in income, you may have options. The Social Security Administration allows individuals to request a reduction in Medicare premiums if the income increase was tied to a qualifying life event (such as the death of a spouse). To request this relief, you'll need to file Form SSA-44 (Medicare Income-Related Monthly Adjustment Amount—Life-Changing Event) and provide supporting documentation. While approval isn't guaranteed, widows may be able to successfully reduce their premiums back to their normal range. This is one more reason to stay proactive and advocate for yourself when navigating these transitions.

If I Downsize, How Can I Invest the Proceeds in a Way that Provides Income without Increasing My Tax Burden?

If you're considering downsizing, one of the most common follow-up questions is: What should I do with the proceeds? More specifically, how can I create income without increasing my tax burden? It's a smart question, and the answer depends on your full financial picture, including your age, income sources, tax bracket, and future goals. The good news is there are tax-efficient ways to generate income from the equity you unlock, whether that means using tax-deferred vehicles, tapping into more conservative income-producing assets, or creating a flexible withdrawal plan that supports both stability and long-term growth. What matters most is that the money you free up by letting go of a costly or oversized home can be reallocated with purpose.

As already stated, downsizing isn't just about square footage. It's about freeing up capital that can support the life ahead with more control, more breathing room, and more peace of mind. In Chapter Three, we'll look at the different ways you can approach investing those proceeds for income, security, and flexibility on your terms.

At some point, the question of selling becomes less about what you're giving up and more about what you're gaining. Downsizing isn't just a financial decision. It's a life decision. And for many widows, it's the beginning of something new filled with more possibility than they ever imagined. Letting go of the house you shared doesn't mean erasing the life you built. It means shaping the life that comes next. It's about rebuilding and creating a life that reflects who you are now, and what you need most going forward.

Maybe that means moving closer to your adult children or grandchildren so you can be present for birthdays, school plays, and impromptu Sunday dinners. Or maybe it means cutting costs, eliminating stairs or reducing yard maintenance. For some, it's about finally living near the beach, golf course, or in the small town they always loved visiting, or just somewhere that feels more manageable and peaceful. Others find joy in a vibrant 55+ community with pickleball courts, walking trails, and neighbors who understand what it means to start over and still thrive.

There's no one right answer, and that's the beauty of it. It's your choice. For some, downsizing can mean upsizing your quality of life. Less to maintain often means more time and energy for what matters. A smaller home can offer greater ease, less cleaning, fewer repairs, and lower stress. It can open the door to travel, new friendships, community involvement, or hobbies you never had time to explore before. And just as important, it gives you a renewed sense of control, choice, and freedom.

But for others, the right move may be to stay. If your home still feels like a place of peace, comfort, and familiarity, that warmth, stability, and a sense of safety may mean you're exactly where you're meant to be. There's no pressure to change something that's still serving you well. Staying in your home can be just as empowering as letting it go, especially when the decision is made intentionally, not out of fear or default. I've had many clients choose to stay, and they've gone on to live deeply contented lives, surrounded by the memories they cherish, within a space that continues to support them both emotionally and practically. So remember, staying is a choice too. And when it's made with clarity, it can feel every bit as liberating.

This isn't about "moving on." It's about moving forward. Your home served you well. Now you have the chance to choose what will support you moving forward. And that choice, made on your terms, can be one of the most liberating, life-affirming steps you take.

WHAT ABOUT RENTING OUT YOUR HOME?

If you're not ready to let go of your home, or if you like the idea of turning it into an income source, you may be considering turning it into a rental. On the surface, this can seem like a win-win. You keep the property, build equity, and generate cash flow. And in some cases, it can be a smart option, especially if the home is in a high-demand area, if you already have experience as a landlord, or if you enjoy the idea (and are okay with the workload) of owning real estate as part of your income strategy.

But before you commit, it's important to look beyond the benefits and consider the realities. First, becoming a landlord is not a passive decision. Even with a property management company (which can charge 8 to 12 percent of your monthly rental income), there will be costs for maintenance and tenant turnover. Even with outsourcing, you are still the one ultimately responsible. That could mean making decisions about repairs, dealing with the cost and stress of unexpected vacancies, covering liabilities as well as staying on top of local rental regulations and tax reporting requirements. If the furnace goes out in December or the pipes burst in the middle of the night, it's your name on the title and your checkbook on the hook. If you don't use a management firm, that dirty work and stress fall directly on your shoulders or requires finding and managing reliable help on your own.

Renting out the home may also mean you're keeping a geographic tie to the area, which could limit your flexibility down the road. If you're dreaming of moving closer to your grandchildren or settling in a community designed for active retirees, a rental property back in your old neighborhood may become more of a burden than a benefit, especially if you need to return for inspections, repairs, or legal issues.

There are tax considerations, too. The moment you turn your home into a rental, it's no longer considered your primary residence. That means if you decide to sell it later, you may lose your eligibility for the $250,000 capital gains exclusion (or $500,000 if you were still within two years of your spouse's death). To qualify again, you would typically need to move back in and live in the home for at least two out of the five years before the sale. That can be complicated, and for some, simply not realistic.

There's also the issue of taxes, which may include reporting across different states if you move or relocate after converting your former home into a rental. Several states will still consider the property taxable in their jurisdiction, and you may be required to file non-resident tax returns and pay state taxes on the rental income, even if you no longer live in that state. And if you eventually sell the property after moving out of state, keep in mind that most states will still tax you on the gain. That's because nearly all states with income taxes impose them on source-based income, which includes rental income and capital gains from real estate physically located within their borders. So even if you move to a no-income-tax state like Florida or Texas, you may still be required to file a non-resident state return in the state where your former home is located.

California, for example, is particularly aggressive in this area. The state will continue to tax you on both rental income and capital gains from the sale of your former property, even years after you've moved away. Selling a home in California as a non-resident means you'll owe tax on the gain, including depreciation recapture, and will need to file a California non-resident return.

But California isn't the only state that does this. New York, Massachusetts, Oregon, and others tax non-residents on rental income and real estate gains tied to properties within their borders. The only real exceptions are the nine states with no personal income tax, such as Florida, Texas, and Wyoming. If your property is located in one of those states, state income tax on the rental income or gain may not apply. But if it's not, you'll likely still have a state tax obligation, based on where the property is located, even if your driver's license and mailing address say otherwise.

This is a common misunderstanding. People often assume that moving out of a high-tax state severs all ties, but when it comes to real estate, the state continues to hold taxing authority over that property. If you're planning to keep your home as a rental and move away, or sell it after relocating, it's crucial to understand the state-level tax consequences, not just the federal rules.

Before you relocate or convert a home to a rental, it's important to understand how your new state and your former state treat the rental income so you're not caught off guard by the double filing requirements or unexpected state tax bills.

Then there's the issue of depreciation. When you convert your former home into a rental, the IRS requires you to depreciate the property. Depreciation is the process of deducting a portion of the property's value each year to reflect wear and tear or obsolescence. For residential real estate, the IRS mandates a depreciation schedule of 27.5 years, which applies only to the structure, not the land. This means that each year, you're expected to deduct a fraction of the dwelling's value from your rental income. This helps lower your taxable rental income and can create significant short-term tax savings.

On the surface, this is an attractive benefit of owning rental property. It's a non-cash deduction that can reduce your tax bill even if you have positive cash flow. But it comes with a catch. When you sell the property, all the depreciation you've taken (or were eligible to take) is recaptured. That means it gets added back into your taxable income and is subject to depreciation recapture tax, which can be as high as 25 percent, regardless of whether the rest of your capital gain is excluded under the home sale exemption. And yes, this recapture applies even if you didn't actually claim the depreciation because the IRS assumes you did.

Example: Depreciation in Real Life

Let's say the value of the dwelling (not including land) on your former home is estimated at $600,000 when you convert it into a rental. The IRS requires that residential real estate be depreciated over 27.5 years. That means each year you must deduct a portion of the home's value. For example, $600,000 ÷ 27.5 years = $21,818 annual depreciation.

For every full year the home is used as a rental, you get to deduct $21,818 from your taxable rental income. Clearly, that's a significant tax benefit. Even if your cash flow is positive, depreciation could allow you to report a much lower (or even negative) taxable income. That is an attractive benefit of rental property ownership. But when you eventually sell the home, all of that depreciation—whether you claimed it or not—must be recaptured and reported as taxable income. It is separate from the capital gain liability due on the property itself. If you rented the home as illustrated above for five years, for example, $109,090 in total depreciation would then be taxed at a maximum federal rate of 25 percent, resulting in up to $27,273 in depreciation recapture tax when you sell.

This surprises many homeowners who thought the home sale exclusion would wipe out all taxes. But depreciation recapture is not excluded, even if the rest of your gain qualifies under the $250,000 (or $500,000) home sale exclusion. That's why it's so important to understand not just the income you might generate from renting, but the tax liability that can follow you later.

What felt like a tax-saving strategy over the years can result in a larger tax bill at the end if not planned for properly. That doesn't mean depreciation is bad, however. It's just something you need to understand going in, especially if you're thinking of renting your home only for a few years before selling. Knowing how depreciation affects your tax picture can help you make a more informed decision about whether renting truly serves your long-term goals.

Finally, while rental income might sound appealing, it's rarely guaranteed. You may have unexpected vacancies or periods where repairs and costs eat up most of what you collect.

Unlike a diversified investment portfolio designed for stable income distributions, rental income can be inconsistent. Some months it may feel like a great source of cash flow. Other times, it may feel like a second job.

All of that said, renting out your home can be part of a well-considered strategy, but it's not always the simple solution people think it is. The key is to go in with your eyes wide open because what sounds good in theory—"I'll just rent it out and let it pay for itself"—often looks very different in practice. Before you pursue that route, ask yourself a few important questions: Do I want to be a landlord right now? Do I want to be tied to this location? Would I be better served emotionally and financially by selling, reinvesting the proceeds, and creating income in a way that doesn't require my time, energy, or physical presence?

There's no right or wrong answer here, except that the best choice is the one that reflects your life now, supports your peace of mind, and aligns with the lifestyle you're intentionally building in this next chapter. This isn't about what feels familiar or what others think you "should" do. It's about what truly serves *you*.

Letting go is giving yourself emotional permission to stop carrying something and honoring that permission with action. You may need time to consider this carefully, and that's okay. The courage to act often comes after clarity settles in.

The question isn't just about real estate or money. It's about your life. Whether you choose to sell, stay, or rent, your decision deserves to be made with thoughtfulness, not fear, and with honesty, not from a feeling of obligation to others or to the past. What you hold on to should support your well-being. What you let go of should make room for something new. You are not the same person as when you bought your home, and the next chapter of your life is unfolding by the day. How you live it is entirely up to you.

CHAPTER FOUR

How to Create an Income Plan

Building a Strategy Designed for One

The picture changed,
but the brush is still in your hand.

A solid retirement plan requires more than just smart investing. It requires a strategy. And when you're planning for one, that strategy needs to be sharper, more deliberate, and fully integrated. Income isn't just a line item when you stop working. It's the foundation of your retirement and the decisions you make now, from when and how you file for Social Security to how you draw from your portfolio, will have a direct impact on your financial security for the decades ahead.

When you're building a retirement income plan for one, there's no room for guesswork. The numbers have to work, month after month, year after year. And not just on paper. They have to work in real life, with all its surprises, needs, and risks. Retirement isn't about maximizing returns anymore. It's about creating consistency, preserving control, and protecting what you've built, because you're the one it all depends on. Retirement for one carries a different weight. Every decision, every dollar, and every trade-off now rests solely on your shoulders.

This is where conversations with your trusted advisors become important. Ideally, you already have a holistic, comprehensive financial and retirement plan in place. But if not, it's time to take action. Retirement is not just about investment allocations and spending, but about how every part of your financial life works together to support your future without a paycheck. Cash flow, taxes, risk, housing, health care, estate planning, asset allocation—they all connect like cogs, propelled by one another. Especially when you are the sole decision-maker and the sole beneficiary, you can't afford to look at these important issues in isolation.

There's no exact timeline for when to begin reshaping your financial life, but as the fog starts to lift, it is time to put pen to paper. If the first 90 days have been about surviving the shock, honoring your grief, and handling immediate logistics, the months that follow are often when reality truly sets in. That's when questions about income, housing, and long-term stability start to feel more urgent. It is also when planning can be not only helpful, but healing. It's not about rushing into decisions or overhauling everything at once. It's about choosing a moment when you feel ready to look ahead, when the fog begins to lift just enough to start thinking about structure, sustainability, and what your life, both financially and personally, needs to look like from here on. That's the time to start. And when you do, it's okay to take it one step at a time. The goal is steady progress, not instant answers.

Ultimately, you need a new strategy that integrates your modified income sources, tax status, and your new lifestyle. Social Security benefits, pensions, rental income, investment withdrawals all need to be evaluated and structured intentionally to support your life now, not the one you shared before. This means making sure your income plan adjusts for taxes, inflation, anticipates your longevity risks, evolves with your goals as you age, and, unfortunately, also accounts for the increasing likelihood of healthcare expenses.

You may also need to simplify the complexity of your finances. That might mean consolidating accounts, organizing your cash flows, or eliminating redundant or outdated holdings. It's not just about cutting clutter. It's about reducing the chances of missed Required Minimum Distributions (RMDs) on IRAs, unintended tax surprises, or overlooked investment risks. Over the years, I've worked with many individuals navigating widowhood who didn't realize how important these steps were until something slipped through the cracks. My team and I have seen accounts left without beneficiaries or incorrectly registered, spousal IRAs not properly set up, and cost basis information that was never updated. These are details that seem small but can undermine financial security. Simplifying doesn't mean sacrificing control. It means refining your financial picture, so everything has a clear purpose. When your financial life is streamlined, your decisions become easier, your plan becomes more resilient, and you're better equipped to stay in control.

Having a sound financial and retirement plan is about moving forward with purpose and financial strength. Whether your loss is recent or years behind you, your financial independence deserves structure, precision, and a holistic plan that reflects your reality. We'll walk through each financial consideration we recommend for our clients, highlight what's different for a single person in retirement, and build toward an income and investment strategy that fits your life now. And while it's possible to navigate this alone, this step is most effective when guided by a professional. I say that not just from experience, but from witnessing how easily overlooked details can slowly erode even the most well-intentioned plans.

Planning for one doesn't mean doing less. It means doing what matters most. It's about clearing the noise and creating a strategy that reflects your reality, your desires, your priorities, and your values. The plan must be reliable, efficient, and built with the understanding that, as with most retirees, there may be no backup plan.

Building that comprehensive, holistic plan step by step starts with first looking at your spending needs. We'll help you break down the steps to align your expenses to your income in a sustainable way. Most importantly, though, you will want to consider every expense you have, both fixed and discretionary, as well as every source of income you may have or need to create: Social Security, pensions, rental income, Required Minimum Distributions and portfolio withdrawals. Next, you will want to review your asset allocation and portfolio management, risk management, longevity, long-term care risks, and how to structure your investments for income and growth with one person in mind—you.

Let's get practical. Let's get precise. Let's build a plan that's not only resilient, but that is truly yours.

RETHINKING CASH FLOW: PLANNING FOR ONE

After the death of a spouse, one of the first and most essential financial steps is reassessing your monthly cash flow. The reality is your income and expenses likely don't look the same anymore. What once supported two people now needs to support one, and that means understanding what's coming in, what's going out, and what changes need to be made to sustain your lifestyle.

Start by creating a baseline. Gather at least 6 to 12 months of household expenses. Look at credit card statements, bank statements, and bill payments to categorize and track spending. Don't rely on memory or assumptions here. The numbers often tell a different story than we expect. You may want to refer to our resources page and download our budget worksheet to help you consider all potential expenses.

Next, categorize each expense into three groups:

1. **Essential Expenses**—housing, utilities, food, insurance, healthcare, transportation.
2. **Lifestyle Expenses**—travel, dining out, hobbies, subscriptions, entertainment.
3. **Discretionary or Occasional Expenses**—gifts, home repairs, pet care, donations, seasonal items.

As painful as it may feel, this is also a chance to streamline. You may find expenses that no longer serve your needs or priorities. For example:

- Housing costs may change if downsizing or relocating is on the table.
- Auto insurance and transportation costs may drop if you no longer need two vehicles.
- Dining, club memberships, or subscriptions geared toward shared activities can often be reduced.
- Life and health insurance premiums tied to your spouse's coverage no longer apply.
- Travel allowance may be reduced or change, especially if they were built around joint experiences.

This is about aligning your spending with your new reality and goals. Your household is different now and so is your budget.

On the flip side, widowhood can introduce new or increased costs you didn't have before:

- Health insurance premiums may rise if you were on your spouse's employer plan and now need to secure your own coverage.
- Professional services such as financial advice, estate planning, or even therapy may become more necessary than ever.
- Home maintenance and repairs might cost more if you're now hiring help for tasks your spouse used to handle.
- Security and technology—from medical alert systems to home monitoring—may be worth considering if living alone changes your safety needs.
- Long-term care planning may take on more urgency. Planning for future care, including in-home help or assisted living, may become a priority.

Once you've broken down your expenses and identified past expenses versus future projections, separate your essential expenses from your lifestyle desires and discretionary expenses. There's no universal rule for what counts as "essential." For some, travel is non-negotiable. For me, my wine club membership makes the list. These decisions are very personal. Even if something seems trivial to others, or like an obvious place to cut back, it may contribute meaningfully to your quality of life. Only you can decide what belongs in which category but be honest with yourself and stay grounded in what's financially realistic. This isn't about restricting your retirement or denying yourself joy. It's about making sure your lifestyle is sustainable over a retirement that could stretch to age 95 or beyond. And with inflation, that future may cost more than you think.

This is one more reason why working with a financial advisor can be invaluable. A qualified planner can help you assess whether your budget aligns with your resources and can run detailed cash flow projections, modeling different inflation rates, market conditions, and life events to stress-test your plan. Retirement happiness isn't just about income. It's about confidence. And confidence comes from knowing your plan holds up for the rest of your life, no matter what happens.

Breaking your budget into three categories—essential, lifestyle and discretionary—can help you determine how to structure your investments. Your essential expenses are non-negotiable. They must be covered regardless of market conditions. Lifestyle expenses are the things that make retirement feel like retirement, such as travel, dining out, hobbies, or family experiences. They're important to your well-being, but not strictly necessary to your survival. Finally, discretionary expenses are the "nice to have's." These expenses can be supported by portfolio growth, or adjusted during leaner times. For example, travel, hobbies, and dining out reflect how you want to live, while luxury upgrades or splurges are truly optional and easiest to scale back if needed.

The next step is to align your income sources with your essential expenses and ensure you have a reliable, sustainable income stream to cover those needs. When you match stability with necessity, you create a foundation that supports both confidence and flexibility in retirement.

Give Yourself Permission to Adjust

Of course, cash flow planning isn't a one-and-done process. It evolves with you. The goal here isn't perfection or austerity. The goal is awareness. You want to know what it takes to support your lifestyle, protect your financial health, and give yourself the flexibility to adapt as life unfolds. The first few months or even the first year after a loss may feel uncertain, and that's okay. What matters is that you take the time to reassess, recalibrate, and give your financial life the structure it needs to support you in the years ahead.

So now is the time to stop reading and get to work on your budget. I know this may still feel overwhelming, especially if you're in the early stages of loss, but this is your moment to pause, reflect, and begin shaping the life that comes next. Take some quiet time and carefully measure what you need, what you value, and try to consider what still brings you joy. As you do this, don't just put on your thinking cap. Try to put on your dreaming cap, too. Imagine your life over the next 10 or 20 years. What's on your bucket list? What experiences or goals are important to you? Start with this simple but powerful question:

Before my time here ends, I want to . . .

INCOME SOURCES

Now that you know what you need, let's review your current income sources. This includes Social Security benefits, pension or annuity payments, rental income, income from employment, investment income, and withdrawals from retirement accounts. This gives you the "inflow" side of the equation.

Start with what's already coming in. Begin with tallying guaranteed income sources that create your base income. Of course, if your loss is recent this may not be accurate since some benefits may be reduced or cease altogether. If that is the case, mark those that may need a revision. If you are working and living off your paycheck, you may have enough to meet your spending needs, but without your spousal income you could find there is a shortfall. Regardless, you will need to take inventory to map out your life plan. Once you total your income from all sources, you can determine how much additional income you need to withdraw from your investment portfolio to bridge the gap, or identify when you might need to start taking withdrawals. Consider:

- employment income
- Social Security benefits
- pension payments
- annuities, if applicable
- rental income or business income

Let's start with a discussion about Social Security, which is one of the only lifetime guaranteed income sources you may have.

SOCIAL SECURITY: WHAT YOU NEED TO KNOW

Social Security was created during the Great Depression and signed into law by President Franklin D. Roosevelt in 1935. It was designed as a safety net, and it was one of the first of its kind in the world. The objective was to provide retired workers with a modest, reliable income after a lifetime of working for a paycheck. Over time, the program expanded to include survivor benefits, disability insurance, and benefits for spouses and children.

Today Social Security continues to serve as the foundation of retirement income for millions of Americans. Despite headlines warning of its "insolvency," the truth is more nuanced. The program is not going bankrupt. Even if no changes are made, which is unlikely, Social Security will still be able to pay about 75 to 80 percent of scheduled benefits after 2033 based on current trust fund projections, as of 2025 Social Security Trustees' Report. That's not ideal, but it's a far cry from disappearing. Congress has options, and the political will to protect this program remains strong, especially given how many Americans depend on it.

In short, Social Security isn't going away. It may evolve, but it remains one of the most stable and essential income sources in retirement planning. The key is to understand the rules and how to maximize your benefits within them.

The Basics: When You Can File and Why Timing Matters

You can begin collecting your own retirement benefit from Social Security as early as age 62, or you can wait until as late as age 70. If you're widowed, you may be eligible to file as early as age 60, but we'll come back to that in a moment. Before you decide when to file, it's essential to understand how Full Retirement Age (FRA) works. Your FRA depends on the year you were born. For most people reading this, it falls between ages 66 and 67. Filing at FRA means you'll receive your full, unreduced Social Security benefit, with no penalty and no earnings restrictions for those who continue working while collecting benefits.

Think about your Social Security filing timeline like a sliding bar that runs from age 62 to 70, with your Full Retirement Age (FRA) marked as a key dot on the bar. If you file before that FRA dot, your benefit gets penalized. It will be reduced for life and you will get smaller cost-of-living increases as a result. Move the slider past FRA, and you earn delayed retirement credits (DRC), which is essentially a bonus of about 8 percent each year that you delay filing up to age 70, which includes increased cost-of-living adjustments.

Please note, this isn't a game of chance. Some people mistakenly see Social Security filing as a bet against the system, a bit like gambling with your life expectancy. But filing is not about making bets. It's about making a strategic decision based on your financial needs, your health, and whether you have the flexibility to delay. Social Security is likely the only source of guaranteed lifetime income you'll ever have, which makes the decision even more important. Rental income, dividends, and investment returns all come with market risk and variability, but Social Security doesn't. That is perhaps the only check you will receive that will keep coming in month after month, year after year, no matter how long you live. And, generally speaking, your first check will likely be the lowest. With cost-of-living (COLA) adjustments, your benefits should rise over time. Consequently, while filing early may offer relief now, filing later can lock in a stronger financial foundation for the long haul. Therefore, understanding where you fall on that timeline, and what each filing point means, is the first step toward maximizing the benefit you've worked so hard to earn.

Filing before your FRA means you'll receive a reduced benefit for life, and that lower amount will also be the baseline for your future COLAs. That means not only is your monthly check smaller, but every future increase will be calculated off that reduced amount. On the other hand, if you delay claiming past your FRA, your benefit will increase by about 8 percent per year until age 70. That growth is in addition to any COLAs, which will be compounded on the higher baseline. Waiting isn't always the right answer, of course, but when you can afford to, it can significantly boost your income for life.

Delayed retirement credits (DRCs) can make a big difference in your long-term income, especially if you live into your 80s or 90s, which is increasingly common these days. Delaying is one of the few ways to guarantee a higher income for life, which is why it's often worth considering if you have other income to live on in the meantime. The trade-off, though, is that if you need income before your age 70, you must draw it from your personal savings and investments. That could ultimately compromise the sustainability of your resources, and since Social Security is not generally enough to live on by itself, you must carefully consider the entire sum of your financial picture. Too many people make Social Security claiming decisions without considering the impact on their total plan.

Survivor Benefits: A Different Path with Its Own Rules

Being widowed means there are different rules. You may be eligible to claim survivor benefits as early as age 60 (or 50 if you are disabled). These are based on your late spouse's earnings record, not your own. This is important to know because claiming survivor benefits doesn't lock you into giving up your own retirement benefit. In fact, you may be able to collect survivor benefits first and let your own retirement benefit grow, earning delayed retirement credits until as late as age 70. Then, you can switch to your higher benefit if it makes sense. Done right, this coordination can significantly boost your lifetime income.

For example, you might take a reduced survivor benefit at 60 or 62 to give yourself income now and then switch to your own benefit at 70 when it's reached its maximum. This approach can help you avoid tapping your investments too early while securing a higher monthly check later in life. It's important to understand that survivor benefits are the only case where you can file for one type of benefit while deferring your own retirement benefit to earn DRCs. However, if you don't have sufficient earnings credits on your own record, this may not be a viable strategy.

If You're Still Working: Know the Earnings Test

If you collect Social Security before your FRA and are still earning income from a job, the earnings test may temporarily reduce your benefit. In 2026, you can earn up to $24,480 without any reduction. If you earn more than that, however, your benefit will be reduced by $1 for every $2 over the limit.

Suppose you start collecting Social Security at age 63 with a monthly benefit of $2,800 while still working. If you earn $60,000 in 2026, your income exceeds the limit by $35,520 ($60,000 – $24,480). The earnings test withholds $1 for every $2 above the limit, which means $17,760 is withheld for the year. At $2,800 per month, that equals just over six months of payments you will not receive in 2026.

This reduction is not permanent, however. Once you reach your Full Retirement Age, your benefit is recalculated to account for what was withheld, and your monthly payment will increase going forward. If you are easing into retirement, working part-time, or consulting before reaching Full Retirement Age, this is an important factor to consider. In some cases, a temporarily reduced benefit can still help bridge income needs without over-relying on savings, but keep in mind that the reduction also applies to survivor benefits.

Benefits for Families with Children

If you're caring for children under age 16, you may be eligible for family survivor benefits as a widow or widower. Your children may also qualify for dependent benefits based on the earnings record of the deceased parent. These benefits can be a critical source of financial support, especially during a time of emotional and financial transition. In some cases, benefits are also available if you're caring for an adult child with a qualifying disability.

It is important to note that these survivor benefits for the widow or widower stop once the youngest child turns 16. Therefore, unless you qualify for another type of benefit, there may be a gap until you become eligible again, which is generally at your age 60 (or age 50 if you are disabled). This gap, often called the "widow's blackout period," can come as a surprise and requires advance planning, since the household income from Social Security may drop significantly during those years.

Social Security: Getting It Right as a Surviving Spouse

Social Security is often one of the first and most important pieces of your income plan to lock in. But when you're widowed, the rules change. As already noted, you may be entitled to your late spouse's benefit. But the details matter, and how you approach this can have a significant impact on your long-term income.

If your spouse had already claimed Social Security before passing, you may be eligible to receive their full benefit or a portion of it, depending on when you file. The amount you receive depends on your age at the time of filing as well as whether your spouse filed before their own Full Retirement Age. If you claim survivor benefits before your FRA, your benefit will be permanently reduced, potentially by as much as 28.5 percent if claimed at the earliest age of 60.

However, as noted earlier, if you're also eligible for your own retirement benefit, you may be able to offset that early-claiming penalty by allowing your own benefit to grow. Filing for the survivor benefit first could let you defer your own benefit to age 70, when you'll receive the full value plus delayed retirement credits. It's a strategy worth reviewing to ensure you're maximizing what you've earned across both records. However, if your spouse claimed their retirement benefits early, say at age 62 or 63, the amount they received was permanently reduced from their full retirement benefit, and that reduced amount now becomes the foundation for your survivor benefit. If you also file early for survivor benefits (before your full retirement age), your benefit is further reduced because of your age. In other words, you could face a "double reduction"—first from your spouse's early claim, and second from your own. This can significantly lower the monthly income you might otherwise have received, so it's essential to understand the timing rules and plan accordingly.

If, however, your spouse passed away before filing, (for example, they passed at age 62) your survivor benefit is based on what they would have received at their FRA, not the reduced amount they might have received if they had filed at the time of their death. That distinction matters. It means their untapped benefit isn't penalized (although, of course, you might receive a penalty if you file before your FRA). As you can see, it's important to structure your strategy carefully to build a stronger foundation for your survivor benefits. In many cases, the right timing strategy can make a six-figure difference over your lifetime.

Some mistakenly believe they can collect both their own benefit *and* a survivor benefit at the same time. That is not true. Instead, you'll receive whichever is higher, or you may be able to claim a reduced survivor benefit early, then switch to your own (higher) benefit later, ideally at age 70 when it's reached its maximum benefit thanks to delayed retirement credits.

Take the case of Clare. When she was 62 her husband passed away unexpectedly, after they had both retired early. She and her husband, Ed, had both worked and had their own Social Security earnings record. But they were planning on delaying filing. Once Ed passed away, however, Clare thought about filing on her record, not knowing about the survivor benefit option. We informed her that claiming benefits early would permanently reduce her monthly benefit as well as her cost of living benefits, and in fact our analysis based on her comprehensive financial plan concluded it could cost her hundreds of thousands of dollars if she lived to her average life expectancy.

Instead, we suggested she use a smarter strategy. Claim a reduced survivor benefit, which provided a modest but reliable income stream, while she adjusted to life on her own. This allowed her to still preserve her investment portfolio, although we did have to generate some income distributions to supplement her survivor benefits. But when she turned 70, she was able to switch to her own full Social Security benefit, which increased substantially thanks to delayed retirement credits, and then reduce her income distributions from her investments. Because she was born in 1952, she received an extra 32 percent on her benefit. (Those born in 1960 or later will be eligible for a maximum of 24 percent DRC.)

By planning it this way, we were able to help Clare avoid unnecessary taxable withdrawals from her IRAs and gave her time to settle into her new rhythm, while ultimately locking in a higher lifetime income later. It's an example of how understanding the rules, and timing your decisions strategically, can lead to significantly better outcomes over the long run.

Now consider Dan, who was in a similar position. His wife passed away after a four-year battle with cancer, and he found himself a widower at age 63. Dan was overwhelmed and unsure of his next steps. Grief made everything foggy, and the pressure of managing finances alone added to the weight. Thinking he had no better option, he claimed his own Social Security benefit right away just to help keep up with the day-to-day expenses. What he didn't realize, and what no one had explained to him, is that he could have claimed a reduced survivor benefit first, allowing his own benefit to grow until age 70. Instead, he unknowingly locked himself into a permanently reduced monthly income, sacrificing thousands of dollars over the course of his retirement. Unfortunately, by the time he came to us, his decision was irreversible and there was no going back. Within just a handful of years, he realized that he was spending down his personal savings faster than he imagined because the modest Social Security benefit just wasn't keeping up with the rising cost of living.

Unfortunately, Dan's story is all too common. In the absence of clear guidance, it's easy to make fast decisions that feel safe in the moment but cost more in the long run. That's why it's so important to understand your options and take the time to plan with a knowledgeable professional who can help you see the full picture before you file.

Survivor benefits are not subject to the deemed filing rule, unlike spousal benefits. In plain English, this means you can choose which benefit to claim first—your own or your survivor benefit. This flexibility is not an option for those who are married and claiming as spouses. But don't assume your local Social Security office will walk you through all the options. They may overlook this so you need to know what to ask for and why.

Finally, if you're still working when you claim a survivor benefit before full retirement age, the earnings test may temporarily reduce your benefit, as described above, but that doesn't necessarily mean it's the wrong move. In fact, for those easing into retirement or cutting back hours, it can still provide valuable income during a transitional period. My mother used survivor benefits to help her fund her 401(k), indirectly, while she worked to age 70 and delayed her filing. That strategy enhanced her lifestyle in retirement quite significantly.

The key is to map out Social Security thoughtfully within the context of a comprehensive financial plan that aligns your goals, your timeline, your tax situation, your resources, and your total financial picture. By now, it should be clear that decisions guided by the full picture, not just the numbers in isolation, you can make choices that truly support your long-term stability and peace of mind.

Bottom line? Social Security planning for surviving spouses is complex, but it's also full of opportunity if you know how to do it right. So before you file, run the numbers. Look at the full picture. Consider how this income fits into your broader plan because once you make a claim, the choice is often permanent.

PENSION BENEFITS

While fewer retirees today have access to traditional pensions, if you or your late spouse do have one, it's critical to understand your income options. Pensions today typically offer a choice between a lump-sum payout or a lifetime monthly income, and your decision can significantly impact your long-term financial security.

If you're the one entitled to the pension, you'll need to decide how to structure your benefit. You may be able to choose a single-life annuity, which provides the highest monthly income but ends at your death, a lump sum payout, which gives you more control but shifts the investment risk to you, or a lifetime income with a guaranteed period, which ensures a minimum number of payments even if you pass away early.

It's important to understand that pensions are generally designed to cover the retiree, and in some cases, a spouse. However, benefits typically do not extend to children or heirs. If you choose a lifetime benefit with, say, a 10-year guarantee and pass away before the end of the 10-year period, the payments will continue to any named beneficiary, including children. But otherwise pension benefits are typically not available to share with your children or a non-spouse. As a single individual filing for a traditional lifetime income benefit, the payments will be guaranteed over your lifetime but stop upon your death, which means even if you only receive one check before you pass away no further payments will be made. In other words, in most cases, your pension cannot be used as part of your legacy plan.

As discussed earlier, inflation is one of the greatest long-term threats to retirement, especially with longevity. So, it's often a catch-22 with pension plans. The income-for-life benefits ensures you don't run out of income, but if your pension does not include cost-of-living adjustments (and most do not, or the plan may not be funded sufficiently to depend on for full cost-of-living adjustments), its purchasing power will likely erode over time, creating financial strain in later years. Choose your benefit option carefully. The right option depends on your life expectancy, income needs today and in the future, and whether leaving a financial legacy is a priority. In many cases, if available, a lump sum offers more flexibility, but it comes with the trade-off. Like a 401(k), there is a risk of running out of income if the assets are not managed carefully.

Now, if your spouse had a pension, your eligibility for survivor benefits depends on the payout option they selected at retirement or as defined by the plan. If your spouse chose a single life benefit, the payments typically stop at their death. However, if they elected a joint and survivor option, a guaranteed term payout or if the plan offers pre-retirement survivor benefits if benefits didn't commence, you may be eligible to receive some or all of the income benefit. It's important to contact the plan administrator to fully understand the benefits you may be entitled to and for how long you can expect to receive them. In most cases, the payout election becomes irrevocable once the claim form is submitted; meaning the decision made at the start of retirement generally cannot be changed. And, in most cases, income benefits won't extend beyond a surviving spouse's lifetime.

If your spouse had not yet filed for their pension benefits at the time of their death, you may have more flexibility. Some plans offer what's known as a qualified pre-retirement survivor annuity, or QPSA, which provides you with monthly income for life, or in some cases a lump sum payout option. The options available to you will depend on the plan's specific rules, whether the pension was from a public or private employer, and how long your spouse was employed under the plan. Because pension elections carry significant long-term consequences, it's essential to review your options carefully with the plan administrator and, if possible, a qualified financial advisor who can help you assess what best supports your long-term financial security in the context of your entire financial picture.

The lump-sum payout option gives you a one-time distribution of your pension's value, which can be rolled into an IRA to defer taxes and invested for long-term growth. This option offers far more flexibility than a traditional pension income benefit. You gain full control over how the funds are invested, how and when income is withdrawn, and who receives the remaining balance after your death. You can tailor your investment strategy to focus on growth, income, or principal preservation, or any combination thereof. You can aim to generate an income stream that keeps pace with inflation. You can also name beneficiaries so that any unused balance can pass directly to your children or heirs, subject to income tax of course. You may even consider using Roth conversion strategies, discussed in Chapter Six, to improve tax efficiency over time.

However, control and flexibility come with a significant trade-off. As noted previously, all of the responsibility shifts to you when you take a lump benefit. You are responsible for managing the portfolio, producing a sustainable income, and ensuring the funds are not depleted too soon. Naturally, in this case it would be prudent to engage a professional to provide assistance, but there are no guarantees when you elect the lump sum payout. While it can be a powerful tool for building wealth and creating a legacy, it does require discipline, planning, risk management, and often professional guidance.

Keep in mind that pension elections are irrevocable once made. That's why it's crucial to review your options carefully, and especially measure the tradeoffs between guaranteed income, flexibility, survivor protection, and tax implications before signing anything. This is a decision that can affect your future retirement.

RENTAL INCOME

Rental property can be a valuable source of retirement income, but it requires a realistic and disciplined approach when incorporating it into your financial plan. Unlike a pension or annuity, rental income is not guaranteed, and the net amount you actually receive can vary widely from year to year. To plan effectively you need to budget for the expenses and disruptions that come with property ownership.

If your spouse handled the finances and you are just diving into this for the first time, start by identifying the gross rental income you expect to receive annually. From there subtract a reasonable estimate for operating expenses, including property taxes, insurance, property management fees (if applicable), maintenance, repairs, utilities (if not covered by tenants), and HOA dues, if applicable. These expenses can add up quickly, and they tend to increase over time.

You'll also need to account for vacancy periods and tenant turnover, which can impact your cash flow. It's not uncommon to experience a month or more without income between tenants, along with cleaning, repairs, or marketing costs to prepare the property for a new lease. A conservative approach is to assume your property will be vacant at least one month out of the year and set aside funds accordingly.

In addition to annual expenses, set aside reserves for capital improvements. These are larger, less frequent costs such as a new roof, HVAC replacement, or major plumbing repairs, but are inevitable expenses when property is held over the long term and should be part of your budget, to avoid surprises.

Another critical consideration is whether you plan to actively manage the property in retirement or hire help. If you don't want the responsibility of managing tenants, handling late-night repairs, or navigating eviction laws, the cost of hiring a property manager (typically 8 to 12 percent of rental income) should be factored in.

Lastly, consider the tax implications of your rental income. Net rental income is generally taxable, though depreciation and other deductions can reduce your taxable income on paper. That said, those tax benefits may shrink over time, and they can create a recapture liability if you sell the property later. Make sure your retirement income plan includes not just the expected rent, but also a plan for taxes, liquidity, and a possible future sale.

If you're considering selling a rental property, take time to explore your options before making any final decisions. A sale can trigger unexpected tax consequences, particularly capital gains and depreciation recapture. Fortunately, there are planning strategies that may help you defer or reduce the tax burden while still relieving you of the ongoing costs and responsibilities of managing the property. The right approach depends on your goals, your timeline, and your broader financial picture. This is the kind of decision that deserves careful consideration. Before moving forward, consult with a qualified financial advisor who can help you evaluate your options and design a plan that works best for you.

Finally, there's the issue of the rising cost of living. Many landlords choose to keep rental increases below market to reduce tenant turnover, and while that may make sense in the short term, the long-term impact on your retirement can be significant. All of your expenses—insurance, taxes, maintenance, HOA dues—will increase over time and that means so will your income needs. If your rental income remains flat, the gap will need to be filled by drawing down more of your personal savings, which should be factored into your projections. The cost to your savings and investments can be substantial over a multi-decade retirement lifetime.

When accounted for properly, rental income can certainly be a valuable piece of your retirement income puzzle, but it is not passive. It requires ongoing attention, reserves for the unexpected, awareness of income erosion, taxes, and a long-term plan for the property itself.

OTHER INCOME

You may have other forms of income that must be factored into your planning. This might include part-time work or consulting income, deferred compensation payouts, trust distributions, business profits, or royalties. Irregular income may require additional cash flow management. Some people receive income from oil, land, or mineral leases, while others may see structured settlements, legal awards, or inheritances that impact their resources later in retirement. These sources can carry unique tax consequences, affect Medicare premiums, or introduce volatility to your plan. The key is to identify each source, understand its timing and reliability, and ensure it's integrated into a broader income and tax strategy.

Once you've taken stock of your cash flow—what's coming in, what's going out, and what's changed—the next step is figuring out how to generate the income you need, not just for this year, but for the years ahead.

BUILDING A SUSTAINABLE WITHDRAWAL STRATEGY

Your investment portfolio becomes the engine that fuels your lifestyle once fixed income sources are accounted for. But withdrawing from your portfolio takes more than just pulling money from wherever it's available. It requires a strategy. The goal is to provide a stable, reliable but rising income to keep up with inflation while preserving your capital and managing taxes.

A general rule of thumb such as the common 4 percent withdrawal rule may be too simplistic. Instead, we prefer to build an income plan that is customized to our clients' needs, because these may vary yearly. You will want an income that adjusts for market volatility (and prevents you from selling low) as well as one that incorporates flexibility and prioritizes tax efficiency, especially now that you're a single filer.

For example, Kate needs $4,000 a month to support her lifestyle after the loss of her husband. She receives $2,000 from Social Security, leaving a $2,000 shortfall that must be covered by her savings. But it's not as simple as withdrawing that amount from her IRA, because IRA distributions are fully taxable as ordinary income. In order for Kate to net $2,000 per month after taxes, she may need to withdraw closer to $30,000 a year from her IRA. Assuming a 20 percent effective tax rate, about $6,000 will go to the IRS, with the remaining $24,000 to supporting her cash flow needs.

That, however, only addresses today's needs. With even modest inflation of, say, 3 percent annually, her monthly income requirement will grow to more than $5,300 in ten years, requiring nearly $64,000 in gross withdrawals from her IRA annually. Over the first ten years, she'll need to draw well over $350,000 from her portfolio, and that's just to maintain her current standard of living. If she lives to age 95, which is consistent with longevity in her family, her retirement income need could exceed $1.5 million in cumulative, inflation-adjusted withdrawals.

Further, if her income need is lower than her Required Minimum Distributions (RMDs), she could be forced to draw down her IRA more quickly than expected once she reaches age 73 (or 75 for those born in 1960 or later). Granted, she could reinvest the unused net proceeds into a taxable account and maintain some growth potential, but it may still amount to far less than she imagined because of taxes. Without modeling the sustainability of her resources considering RMDs, she may not fully grasp the long-term impact. Many people spend their RMDs without realizing how it accelerates the depletion of their retirement accounts.

You see? Planning your income strategy is not just about covering next month's bills. It's about understanding where your income will come from, how it will be taxed, how inflation erodes purchasing power, so you can anticipate future needs and determine whether your portfolio is designed to sustain you through the decades ahead. Only then can you really identify what you need to do proactively to support the sustainability of your savings.

Retirement planning, especially after the loss of a spouse, is not a do-it-yourself exercise. It's not just about plugging numbers into a calculator and hoping the outcome holds true for the next 30 years. While there are plenty of free tools online that offer basic projections, most fail to account for the real-world complexity of taxes, inflation, changing expenses, market volatility, Social Security coordination, and shifting income needs over time. More comprehensive planning typically requires integrating these variables into detailed cash-flow modeling and stress testing across different scenarios, rather than relying on a single set of assumptions. Working with a qualified financial professional who understands how these moving parts interact can help ensure decisions are evaluated in context, not isolation, and that plans are built around real-world tradeoffs rather than idealized outcomes. But keep in mind, this kind of personalized guidance typically involves a professional fee. What matters most is that you're working with a qualified advisor who puts your interests first and is transparent about how they're compensated. In many cases, that means choosing someone who is not incentivized by commissions on the advice they provide but instead serves as a fiduciary in every aspect of the relationship.

Generating Income for Life

One of the most common fears after losing a spouse is the fear of running out of money. The responsibility can feel heavier now, more personal, more urgent because it sits squarely on your shoulders. You may lie awake wondering, *Do I have enough? Will I be okay?* Those thoughts are completely valid. But it's important to remember that while the fear may feel greater now when you are on your own, the actual financial risk is often lower. Supporting one life is different than supporting two. The cost of healthcare, housing, travel, and even food shifts. The math changes, but in many cases it changes in your favor.

What doesn't change is the need for a sustainable income plan. You still need consistent, reliable cash flow that can support your lifestyle today and adjust for the future. That means creating an income strategy that's flexible, tax-efficient, and built to last. It's not just for the next year, but for the decades ahead.

There are several ways to generate income in retirement. For instance, you may rely on a mix of interest and dividends from your portfolio. However, it's nice to have a steady income stream that, when managed well, can supplement Social Security or a pension even if interest rates change and dividends go down. That is why setting up systematic withdrawals from your investment accounts can prove to be more efficient. When the focus shifts from accumulation to careful distribution, timing and coordination matter. The goal is to take what you need, when you need it, while minimizing taxes and preserving longevity. Again, I must reiterate that tackling this without the help of a professional can be risky. That's because retirees risk withdrawing more than their portfolio can afford to sustain, either by miscalculating rate of return assumptions, failing to consider a sustainable withdrawal rate based on their life expectancy, or failing to account for things like taxes and inflation. Inflation plays a bigger role than most realize. Your income strategy needs to account for rising costs over time, especially if you want to maintain your standard of living. That means building in growth, not just safety, into your investment decisions. A conservative approach can erode your buying power just as surely as a bad stock market can.

A sustainable withdrawal rate depends on your asset allocation structure, investment performance, risk, and outcomes. Further, it can vary based on income needs that can fluctuate. Rarely do I see these needs as a consistent figure, even when adjusted for inflation. For instance, suppose you need $5,000 a month today, but once you file for Social Security, you only need $3,000 a month. Then periodically you may need to take out more for travel, a new car, or home improvement costs. How do you translate that into a fixed withdrawal rate?

For this reason, I find the "4 Percent Rule"—which suggests withdrawing 4 percent annually from your savings in order to preserve your savings over your lifetime—to be far too generic and often inefficient for our clients' needs. The end result is that you could spend more than necessary or still risk running out of money if you don't manage your income strategy, taxes, and investment portfolio diligently. While most of us would like to keep it simple, the complexities of retirement these days often prohibit simplicity.

What matters most is that your income plan is coordinated across your accounts, your tax picture, and your evolving needs. Retirement isn't just about *what* you've saved. It's about *how you use it*. And when you have a clear, disciplined income strategy in place, you don't have to live in fear of running out. You get to live with confidence on your own, and on your own terms.

WHAT ABOUT ANNUITIES?

No discussion of retirement income would be complete without addressing annuities. But let me be upfront. In my experience, some annuity contracts can be overly complicated, carry higher fees, and may not always align with an investor's long-term goals. While annuities are often presented as tools for generating guaranteed income and providing financial security, we've found that some may deliver lower than expected returns, offer limited liquidity, or include features that are difficult to understand. In specific instances, the structure of the contract may not provide the long-term value that investors anticipate.

That said, I also know that annuities are a component of many retirees' portfolios. Sometimes they are purchased when market risk and uncertainty are a concern. So let's talk objectively about what annuities are, what role (if any) they can play in a surviving spouse's income plan, and what to consider if you already own one.

At their core, annuities are contracts with an insurance company. You provide a lump sum of money, and in return the insurer agrees to make periodic payments, either immediately or in the future. These payments may be designed to last for a set number of years or for the rest of your life. For those concerned about longevity risk, this structure can provide a level of income predictability. But of course these lifetime benefits typically come with costs and limitations.

Some annuities offer income riders that can provide guaranteed income while allowing you continued access to the underlying contract value, or your savings balance. But others may require full annuitization, meaning you exchange your lump sum savings for an income benefit, often giving up access to your savings. Income annuities can be a way to turn your savings into a pension-like benefit, but keep in mind that these income decisions can be irrevocable and there are trade-offs to every option.

Because annuities are complex and carry long-term implications, it's important to evaluate them within the broader context of your retirement income strategy. A qualified financial advisor can help you understand how the contract's features, costs, and guarantees align with your goals, risk tolerance, and tax situation. However, consider working with an advisor who is a fiduciary (which means they are legally obligated to act in your best interest), rather than one who stands to benefit from a commission if you purchase the annuity. You may want to get a second opinion since these are serious decisions, but be sure you work with someone who can explain the potential trade-offs without the pressure of a product sale.

Unfortunately, annuities are frequently misunderstood and need to be evaluated carefully. Annuities may come with many features, and it's easy to see the appeal. They can offer guaranteed lifetime income, tax-deferred growth, principal protection, and customizable payout options. Some contracts also include bonuses or premium enhancements, death benefit guarantees, and optional long-term care riders. Others offer inflation-adjusted income and structured payout options. Annuities can also help avoid probate and, depending on your state, may offer creditor protection. Certain products include riders like a guaranteed minimum withdrawal or income benefits (GMWB and GMIB), which can offer retirees a sense of security through more predictable cash flow. But these benefits come at a considerable cost.

Beyond the mechanics, annuities can also provide a psychological benefit. For income annuities, there is peace of mind that comes with income certainty. However, annuities also can be layered with restrictions, including limited liquidity, surrender charges for early withdrawals, caps on growth potential, and/

or complex formulas that determine how much of the market upside or downside protection you actually receive. Riders that promise income guarantees or enhanced benefits may carry additional costs that can erode account values. Bonus interest rates can come at the expense of lower-than-average rates later on, or higher surrender charges. The appeal of safety and predictability may come at the expense of flexibility and longer-term opportunity. That's why it's essential to understand exactly what you're buying, how it fits into your overall plan, and whether the trade-offs are appropriate for your needs.

One important consideration is the commitment of your money. Some contracts carry surrender charges that can last for a decade or more. This means that if you change your mind or need access early, withdrawals may be limited (often to 10 percent a year) or subject to significant penalties, depending on the contract.

It's also important to recognize that income benefits typically do not keep pace with inflation. In addition, income riders often draw from your account value first, with the insurance company's guarantees applying only if your own savings are depleted. Over time, fees and expenses can erode growth, which may cause you to spend down principal more quickly than expected. Combined with surrender charges, this can make changing course difficult or less effective

Examine the guarantees carefully. They may offer a payout that is substantially less than what some investors could generate through a diversified investment portfolio, depending on their goals and market conditions. Every investment decision involves trade-offs, and annuities are no exception. They are often marketed with attractive features, but those features can carry significant limitations that need to be weighed. Of course there is no perfect solution but given that annuities are contracts, the details matter so read the fine print.

I recommend you always ask the difficult questions and review all other options before committing to an annuity purchase. Like any tool, an annuity should only be used if it clearly fits your needs.

For non-retirement accounts (also called nonqualified accounts), annuities offer tax-deferred growth, which can be an appealing feature. Investment earnings compound without current taxation, and taxes are not due until funds are withdrawn. For example, if you sold your home and had $500,000 in proceeds to invest and you didn't need current income, you might consider a nonqualified annuity because it allows earnings to accumulate tax deferred. Unlike IRAs or 401(k)s, which also offer tax deferral but have annual contribution limits, annuities do not cap the amount you can contribute.

That said, tax deferral does not mean tax-free. Withdrawals from nonqualified annuities are generally taxed as ordinary income rather than capital gains, and distributions can increase reported income in the year they are taken. As a result, annuities may create tax considerations later, particularly for widows managing income thresholds tied to Medicare premiums or Social Security taxation.

When you purchase a deferred annuity you can choose to earn a fixed rate or invest in subaccounts (mutual fund-like investments that provide diversification similar to a 401(k)). Regardless of how much you earn, no taxes are reported or due on investment gains. That is, until you take a withdrawal. This feature can be valuable for individuals in higher tax brackets, although it should be weighed alongside the costs, liquidity restrictions, and other terms of the contract, of course.

Perhaps the most important thing to understand is that once you do take a withdrawal, the tax treatment changes. Withdrawals are taxed on a 'last in, first out' (LIFO) basis, meaning that earnings are considered to come out first. Those earnings are taxed at ordinary income tax rates, which are often higher than the long-term capital gains rates applied to many investments. Suppose your $500,000 grew to $1 million. You would pay ordinary income tax rates on the first $500,000 in withdrawals.

By comparison, if you invested in a stock portfolio for $500,000 that grew to $1 million, like the annuity you would not owe taxes on the gain until you sold shares, and at that point the gain would generally be subject to long-term capital gains tax rates, which are typically lower than ordinary income rates.

As a result, annuities may increase your overall tax burden. You may also have some flexibility over which shares are sold, allowing gains to be managed over time rather than recognized all at once. It is important to evaluate not only the tax deferral benefit of annuities, but also the tax treatment when funds are eventually withdrawn. Further, annuities also do not receive a step-up in cost basis at death. That means that if you defer the earnings in nonqualified annuity and never take distributions, your heirs will likely owe ordinary income tax on all the gains. A brokerage account holding stocks or mutual funds, by comparison, typically benefits from a step-up in basis, which means your heirs may have no tax liability on the gains. Therefore, when evaluating the after-tax impact of annuities, especially in light of internal costs, liquidity limitations, and inflation concerns, it's important to assess how they stack up against other income and investment options overall.

Nonetheless, annuities represent a significant part of the retirement product landscape, with trillions invested across various contract types. In my experience working with thousands of retirees, I have observed that annuity contracts, particularly those with multiple riders, higher internal costs, or limited liquidity, can carry features and restrictions that are not fully understood by contract owners. Being aware of these costs and limitations is essential to evaluating whether an annuity aligns with your retirement strategy.

If you already own an annuity, the most important step is understanding the details. Annuity contracts can vary, and even those issued by the same insurance company may have substantially different terms, benefits, and costs. Annuities come in many forms, from fixed, variable to indexed, and immediate to deferred, and every contract has its own terms. Some may continue to serve your needs, especially if they've moved beyond surrender periods or are providing stable income. But in other cases, you might consider changes such as starting regular income payments from the annuity, using a 1035 exchange to move into a different contract without triggering taxes, or exploring ways to access more of your money to better support your evolving retirement plan. I always tell clients if the goal is retirement income, we will look at all available options side by side, and assess which approach offers the best combination of predictability, tax efficiency, access, and alignment with your current goals.

The bottom line is that annuities can produce very different outcomes depending on the specific contract and how it is used. Because they are often long-term contracts with significant complexity, it is easy to misunderstand the benefits, which is why they deserve careful attention. Whether an annuity makes sense depends entirely on your goals, income needs, and overall financial picture. For some retirees, a well-structured, tax-aware income strategy may provide greater flexibility and control; however, what matters most is understanding what you own, why you own it, and whether it still supports the retirement you envision.

ASSET ALLOCATION THAT ALIGNS WITH YOUR INCOME NEEDS

Widowhood may change how your investments should be structured. The portfolio that made sense when you were part of a couple may not reflect your new reality. You now need to revisit your asset allocation with fresh eyes, making sure your investments are aligned to support your lifestyle, your income needs, and your risk tolerance, not the joint needs you had, with joint life expectancies, joint risks, and joint challenges. Major life changes often require a reassessment of how your portfolio is structured.

One of the biggest shifts may be in your risk profile. If you were a growth-oriented investor as a couple, you may feel less comfortable with volatility when you're managing money alone. The emotional weight of market losses can feel heavier, and the desire for predictability often increases when there's no longer a second income or second opinion in the household. That doesn't mean eliminating growth assets altogether, but it does mean you need a more careful, intentional structure.

Your income needs may also have changed. You might be drawing from your portfolio to support yourself rather than reinvesting dividends or deferring withdrawals. That means your portfolio ought to be designed to generate steady, reliable income without putting you in a position where you're forced to sell investments at the wrong time just to pay the bills.

And we can't ignore the time horizon. When you were planning for two lives, you were likely using the longer of the two life expectancies. Now the focus is solely on your life expectancy, and possibly your legacy goals. This may change the calculus for how long your money needs to last, how much risk you can reasonably take, and how you prioritize cash flow versus growth.

A practical way to bring all these elements together is what's often referred to as a bucket strategy. Think of your portfolio not as one big pool of money, but as a series of distinct segments, or buckets, each designed with a purpose and a timeline in mind. Your short-term bucket, for example, holds the money you'll need in the next one to three years. This is your safety net. It might include cash, high-yield savings accounts, certificates of deposit (CDs), or short-term bonds. These assets don't earn much, but that's not their job. Their role is to preserve capital and provide stability, not growth. Because they don't fluctuate much in value, they give you peace of mind and reliable access when you need it most.

When we manage money for clients who are living off their portfolio, we generally aim to keep at least two full years' worth of income needs in this short-term bucket. Why? Because we want to make sure we are never in a position where we have to sell investments during a market downturn just to help the client pay bills. Two years gives us breathing room. If the market is falling, we have time to let the rest of the portfolio recover while still meeting their fixed income needs. This isn't just about comfort, of course; it's a critical strategy to help reduce what's known as *sequence of return risk.*

Sequence risk is one of the most dangerous and misunderstood risks in retirement. It's not just about your average return over time. It's about the order, or sequence, of those returns. If the market drops significantly in the early years of your retirement and you're forced to withdraw from your portfolio at the same time, you can do long-term damage that's hard to recover from. But if you have a short-term bucket to draw from instead, you can ride out the volatility without selling your long-term investments and locking in market losses. It's a simple, practical safeguard that can make a major difference in the longevity of your portfolio.

Your mid-term bucket is for money you won't need immediately but which you may tap into in the next three to seven years. This part of your portfolio can include bonds, conservative balanced funds and high-quality dividend-paying stocks. The goal is to focus on investments that still carry some risk but aim for modest growth and higher income to keep up with inflation and ahead of taxes while protecting against major market swings. This bucket also gives your long-term investments time to grow, while providing you with flexibility and stability. Earnings from this bucket generally feed into your short-term bucket to keep that fluid.

Finally, there's your long-term bucket. This is the portion of your portfolio that won't be touched for at least seven years and is therefore positioned for long-term growth. This is where you might hold a well-diversified stock portfolio, real estate investment trusts (REITs), or other growth-oriented investments designed to keep pace with or outpace inflation. This bucket is crucial because retirement isn't a short-term event. You may need to plan for another 25 or 30 years, and over that time inflation can quietly erode your purchasing power unless part of your portfolio is still growing.

The beauty of this structure is that it helps you stay invested without panicking. When markets fall, you're not scrambling to sell your long-term investments to cover short-term needs. Instead, you can draw from your stable, short-term bucket while giving your growth assets time to recover. It's a strategy rooted in discipline, not reaction. Just as importantly, this kind of strategy brings emotional clarity. You're no longer reacting to headlines or trying to guess whether the market will go up or down next week. You have a strategy. And having a strategy is smart and deeply reassuring. It takes the uncertainty and second-guessing off your shoulders and replaces it with intention.

Whether you follow the strategy we use with our clients, one you develop on your own, or one your advisor recommends, the key is that you have a plan. You do not want to maintain an investment portfolio without an income plan because, in the absence of forethought, you risk reacting to economic or market disruptions in a way that could cause irrevocable harm to your retirement security. You need an income plan that addresses both your current and future needs. The cost of living will continue to rise, so be mindful that what seems like enough today may not be enough tomorrow. Without a strategy that accounts for growth, income, and inflation, you run the risk of outliving your assets.

Of course, there is value in active portfolio management. At times a passive investment style can be rewarding, particularly in strong bull markets. However, market performance is often influenced by factors such as monetary policy, tax law changes, business cycles, geopolitics, and Federal Reserve actions. These forces can drive results in market segments that are not always easily accessible to individual investors. For these reasons, professional management may provide benefits by helping investors navigate complexity and identify opportunities within a broader investment landscape.

Portfolio management on its own can add value, but when paired with comprehensive planning it becomes far more powerful. Planning provides the framework to determine how investments should be used to support income needs, manage taxes, and protect against risks over time. In this way, professional management combined with thoughtful planning can enhance and optimize the retirement journey, helping ensure that the portfolio is not just managed, but managed with purpose.

Planning gives you control, confidence, and the ability to move forward on your terms with peace of mind. Of course, no two situations are identical, so your investment allocation should be based on your lifestyle, your legacy goals, and your comfort level, not a generic model which some firms rely on. Maybe you want to preserve wealth for your children or grandchildren. Maybe you want to give to causes that matter to you or honor your spouse. Or maybe you simply want the assurance that you will not outlive your money. That is why planning matters. When your investments are aligned with your values and your goals, it becomes easier to move forward with conviction, direction, and purpose.

When it comes to asset allocation, there's no one-size-fits-all formula. Your mix of stocks, bonds, and cash should reflect your risk tolerance, time horizon, income needs, financial plan, and emotional comfort. Above all else, it should make sense relative to the current market conditions. That said, it can be helpful to look at a few simplified examples of how portfolios might be structured at a basic level, just to understand the general framework.

For someone newly widowed in their late sixties who needs income right away and has a moderately low risk tolerance, a balanced allocation might look something like 50 percent in bonds and income producing investments, 35 percent in equities, and 15 percent in cash or cash equivalents. This gives them the ability to generate steady income, maintain some growth exposure to keep pace with inflation, and have a cushion for near-term needs. Another person, perhaps younger, say in their late fifties, with no immediate need for income and a stronger stomach for market volatility might lean more growth oriented. They might hold 65 percent equities, 25 percent bonds, and 10 percent cash. This allocation offers more growth potential over the long term but still includes income-generating investments and a cash buffer for emergencies or planned withdrawals.

On the other end of the spectrum, someone in their mid-seventies who is primarily focused on stability and rising income withdrawals, might hold 50 percent bonds, 40 percent equities, and 10 percent in cash. This mix can reduce portfolio swings while still aiming to outpace inflation over time, particularly through high quality dividend stocks and intermediate term bonds. Then again, someone in their eighties who does not need any income from their portfolio and is mostly concerned about taxes, longevity risk, and generational planning might have as much as 65 to 70 percent in equities.

These are just examples meant to illustrate the logic behind diversified investing. What is missing from this consideration, however, are your individual needs and the current market conditions. While no one truly wants risk—after all, who wants to lose money?—there is always a tradeoff between risk and return. For example, for a newly widowed woman in her late sixties who needs to earn a 6 percent return on her portfolio to meet her income needs, and who expects to live to age 95, a more conservative portfolio could fall short of that objective. While low volatility may be ideal, the long-term consequence could be the gradual erosion of her savings.

Now add market conditions into the mix. If the Federal Reserve is raising interest rates, a greater allocation to fixed income might help you reach your goal with less risk. On the other hand, if the economy is in recession and interest rates are cut while stock prices are depressed, increasing stock exposure could provide better long-term results for the same relative risk. Asset allocation is not a set-and-forget exercise; it is a tool that must adapt. The real question is whether you would rather weather market swings or risk running out of money. Too many retirees focus only on their age or general risk tolerance, without accounting for the market risks and opportunities at a given time, or their personal rate of return needed to sustain retirement on their terms.

At the same time, if your plan relies on an unrealistic return—say, 8 to 10 percent—to cover your projected expenses over a long retirement, you may be setting yourself up for disappointment. I have seen people assume more risk than their goals require, and others invest too cautiously in reaction to market headlines, without considering the long-term impact to their portfolio's sustainability. The challenge is not choosing between growth and safety. The challenge is balancing the two in a way that supports your needs today while positioning you for success over the years to come.

The higher your net worth, the more sophisticated your portfolio should become. At a certain level of wealth, investing is no longer just about asset allocation. It becomes a matter of asset integration, tax strategy, and the thoughtful use of tools not typically available through a do-it-yourself platform. This may include hedging strategies for downside protection, real estate investment trusts for income and inflation buffering, or private equity and private debt for growth beyond traditional markets for those who qualify as accredited investors. If you hold concentrated stock positions or legacy business interests, you may need customized risk management strategies such as derivative overlays to mitigate exposure without triggering unwanted taxes. Sophisticated investing is not about chasing past performance or being speculative. To the contrary, it's about precision and alignment. The more moving parts in your financial life, the more carefully they must be managed.

Above all else, asset allocation is a strategy that should support your goals and balances current market risks and opportunities with long-term positioning. At its core, it's about designing a portfolio that reflects you—your stage of life, your income needs, your objectives, and your long-term vision. Widowhood changes all of that, and your portfolio should change with it. A thoughtful allocation provides structure in uncertain times, creating space between you and the daily noise of the markets. Whether you're using a simple three-bucket strategy to balance short-term income with long-term growth, or you've reached a level of wealth that calls for more advanced tools, the goal is the same. It's to build a portfolio that supports your lifestyle, optimizes investment potential while minimizing the risk of large losses, reduces emotional decision-making, is tax efficient, and gives you confidence in your financial future. You don't have to get every detail right on day one, but you do need a plan that evolves with your needs.

The Big Picture

Generating income in retirement after the loss of a spouse isn't just about *how much*. It is also about where the income comes from, when it's taxed, and how long it lasts. Your income strategy should give you both confidence and control, not just cover your bills today. With the right structure in place, you can have both stability and flexibility, both of which become even more valuable when you're planning for one instead of two.

Building that kind of plan begins with understanding your Social Security options and evaluating any other income, such as rental and pension income. Asset allocation plays an equally important role, not only in managing risk and return, but in providing emotional grounding during a time of enormous change. What matters now is that you take the pieces we've discussed and bring them together into a plan that supports your life today, tomorrow, and in the decades ahead.

Widowhood is the end of one chapter and the beginning of another. From here forward, the financial decisions are yours to make. Done well, an income plan doesn't just provide money. It provides stability and freedom. You deserve the freedom that allows you to move forward on your own terms.

However, as I've stated before, you don't have to do it alone. There are numerous options available to help you, but you do need to take ownership of the process. Your future isn't something to be feared, even if it seems like an impossible task. The word itself—impossible—says *I'm possible!* as Audrey Hepburn once said. Understand that your future is something to be *designed,* with wisdom, intention, and a plan that honors who you are now and everything you've done to get here.

CHAPTER FIVE

How to Update Your Estate Plan

Making Sure Everything Reflects Your Life Today

What you've built deserves protection.
What you value deserves a voice.

The death of a spouse changes more than your emotional world. It changes your legal, financial, and logistical life as well. And although no one wants to spend time sorting through paperwork while still grieving, your estate plan needs to be revisited. It's not about erasing the past. It's about protecting your future.

Updating your estate plan is not something you need to do in the first week or even the first month after losing your spouse. Grief takes time, and no one expects you to dive into legal and financial paperwork while you're still absorbing the weight of loss. In fact, it could be a big mistake rushing into major projects, as already addressed. That said, when you're ready to face the details, taking action with your estate plan becomes one of the most empowering and protective steps you can take for yourself, for those you care about, and for everything you've worked so hard to build.

Most of us spend a lifetime accumulating assets, such as homes, savings, investments, personal belongings and retirement accounts. But far too few spend time deciding, clearly and formally, what should happen to those assets upon their death or incapacity. In fact, many people spend more time planning their vacations than they do on their estate plan. And while it's easy to put off, this is not a task that should be left to chance or for others to decide.

Estate planning is about far more than dividing your possessions after you're gone. It's about making sure you're protected while you're still here. It's about maintaining control over your own decisions in moments when you may not be able to voice them yourself. If you want a say in who will manage your finances if you're hospitalized, or who will speak on your behalf if you can't communicate your health care preferences, then you need an estate plan. This is your life and if you want a say in how it unfolds and how it concludes, then your desires must be written down, legally recognized, and up to date.

An estate plan will also reduce unnecessary confusion, stress, and conflict for your loved ones. It can help minimize expenses, avoid probate delays, and ensure that your wishes are clear, rather than assumed. It's the difference between your family having to guess about your wishes versus your family being guided. It's the difference between scrambling and making hasty decisions versus carefully executing a well-thought-out plan.

As a surviving spouse, your priorities may have changed. You may now have different goals, responsibilities, or relationships to consider. What you once planned jointly may now need to be adjusted independently. It's not about erasing your shared history, of course. But it is about updating your legal and financial world to reflect your current reality. It's about honoring the life you've lived, while safeguarding the life that lies ahead.

Whether you already have a plan in place or are starting from scratch, there are key areas to review, decisions to revisit, and details to organize. Estate planning isn't just about completing documents, it is about gaining peace of mind and putting your life in order in a way that reflects where you are today. You'll find that updating your estate plan isn't just a task, it's a powerful declaration that your life still matters, your voice still matters, and your wishes deserve to be honored.

WHY UPDATING MATTERS—EVEN IF YOU THINK YOU'RE "SET"

Many people believe that once they have a will or trust in place, they're done. They check the box, put the binder on a shelf, and move on, relieved to have it "handled." But estate planning is not a one-time event. It's not a static document. It's a living, evolving framework that must reflect your life as it changes, and as your relationships, your values, your responsibilities, and your wishes change. After the loss of a spouse, much of what once made sense in your estate plan may no longer fit. Your priorities may have changed. Your beneficiaries may need to be updated. The person you once trusted to handle financial or medical matters may no longer be the right choice. Your financial circumstances have changed in a meaningful way, from taxes and income to liquidity and asset ownership, and as a result it may become even more important to make sure your documents reflect the reality of your current situation.

Letting old documents linger without review can create real risk. Outdated plans can lead to unnecessary delays, costs, incorrect distributions, probate headaches, or confusion about your true intentions. In the worst cases, it can lead to family conflict, legal disputes, or your wishes being overridden by default laws. And when these things happen, they often do so during emotionally raw times, compounding stress when simplicity is needed most. That's why updating your estate plan isn't just about being organized. It's about protecting your peace of mind. It's about taking control. And it's about making life easier for the people who may one day need to step in and carry out your wishes. It's an act of love for yourself and for the people who matter most to you. This process is about intentionally stepping forward because sometimes the real consequences of waiting too long don't show up until it's too late.

WHY WAITING CAN COST MORE THAN YOU THINK

Several years ago I worked with a client we'll call Margaret. When Margaret's husband passed away, she intended to update her trust but never quite got around to it. Life was busy, and since she had already set up an estate plan years earlier with her husband, she assumed she was "set."

Fast forward 15 years. Margaret developed dementia. Her appointed successor trustee, someone she had thoughtfully chosen years ago, needed to step in and help manage her affairs. But there was a problem. No one could locate the trust documents. Everything was titled in the name of her trust. Her bank accounts, her property, her investment accounts were owned by her trust, just as it should have been, but without the document her trustee had no legal authority to access them. That meant he couldn't withdraw funds to pay her assisted living costs. The attorney who created the trust (and who normally would store copies) had retired and could not be located.

What followed was a complicated, stressful process. It took nearly three months of working closely with our estate attorney to recreate enough legal authority to allow her successor trustee to act on her behalf. During that time, her investment portfolio could not be properly managed, and her home could not be sold. Meanwhile, bills, including the cost for her nursing home, had to be paid out of pocket by the family. Her care could have been compromised had her family not been able or willing to step in financially. Needless to say, it was an emotional time for all involved. Without the estate attorney's diligence and full cooperation of the successor trustee, Margaret's assets could have ended up locked up in court, requiring a conservatorship petition, and possibly draining her resources through legal fees.

Margaret had intended to protect herself. She had taken the first step years ago. But by not updating her plan after her husband's death, and by not making sure everything was accessible and current, she unknowingly left herself vulnerable at a time when she needed protection the most.

REVISITING THE WILL: WHAT NEEDS TO CHANGE?

Gallup polling has found that slightly less than half of U.S. adults, about 46 percent, have a will, with Americans aged 65 and older more likely to have one. Your will outlines your final wishes such as who receives what, who settles your estate, and how your property is handled after your passing. Whether or not you have a will, after losing your spouse, there are specific items you'll want to review carefully, update, or change to ensure your estate plan still reflects your wishes and circumstances.

First, you will need to revisit your choice of executor, also known as your personal representative. If your spouse was originally named, you'll need to appoint a new individual to serve in this important role. An executor is responsible for carrying out the terms of your will, working with the probate court, managing distributions, and ensuring that debts and taxes are settled. It goes without saying that you need to choose someone you trust.

You'll need someone capable, responsible, and willing to take on what can be a significant responsibility at an emotionally challenging time.

You should also take time to review your list of beneficiaries. The people or organizations you originally intended to inherit your assets may need to be updated now that your circumstances have changed. You will want to remove your spouse's name and may want to adjust distributions among children or grandchildren, add new beneficiaries such as charities, or even revise the shares different beneficiaries receive. Beneficiary designations reflect your relationships and priorities, and those can evolve after the loss of a spouse.

In addition to general beneficiary updates, it's important to reconsider any specific bequests you included in your original will. Items such as family heirlooms, property, jewelry, or other personal effects of financial value might now be distributed differently based on the relationships and needs of those around you. What once made sense when you and your spouse made these decisions together may no longer match the realities of your family dynamics today.

If you still have minor children or dependent adults under your care, updating guardianship provisions is also critical. If your spouse was named as the primary guardian, you will now need to appoint someone else. Choosing a new guardian is one of the most personal and difficult decisions in estate planning, but it ensures that the people you love most will be cared for according to your wishes.

Even if you find upon review that your will does not need significant substantive changes, it is often wise to re-sign and re-date it to avoid any potential confusion about which version is operative and ensure that the document clearly reflects your current intentions and authority.

As important as a will is, it is equally important to understand what a will can and cannot accomplish. Many people mistakenly believe that having a will in place means their estate will avoid probate. Unfortunately, that is not the case. In fact, a will directs the probate process. When an individual dies, the court must step in to validate the will, identify the assets that individual owned, determine any outstanding debts, and oversee the distribution of assets to the rightful beneficiaries. Therefore, probate is the legal process of settling an estate. The process is far more involved than you may realize, and it is very public.

First, an obituary must typically be published to publicly announce the individual's passing. This serves as legal notice, giving creditors and anyone who believes they have a claim against the estate an opportunity to come forward. Once that step is complete, the probate court will determine whether a will exists and, if so, whether it is legally valid.

This is where things can get complicated, because wills are often contested. If a will is ambiguous or if someone challenges its legitimacy, the court must evaluate its validity as a whole. The court cannot simply select certain portions of the will to enforce while discarding others. It's an all-or-nothing proposition. For example, if a neighbor comes forward to the probate court and claims your spouse verbally promised him his truck, but the written will makes no mention of this gift, the court must determine whether the claim introduces ambiguity. If the court finds the will to be unclear and the ambiguity is material, meaning it affects the interpretation of the will's core terms, the court may rule the entire will invalid. If the neighbor's claim is found to have no merit and lacks supporting evidence, the court will likely disregard the claim, but not before delays with legal review and possibly litigation have been exhausted.

Ambiguity in a will can also be the result of poorly drafted or conflicting language within the document itself. For instance, if a will states, "I leave my home to my children," but later refers to "the house on Maple Street going to my eldest son," without clarifying which property is defined as "my home," this kind of contradiction can create confusion about the decedent's true intent. If the court is unable to resolve the ambiguity through evidence or reasonable interpretation, the estate may be distributed according to state intestacy laws, essentially treating the decedent as though they died without a will at all, which means their legacy wishes may be compromised.

The probate process often involves legal fees, court filings, required notices to potential creditors, and mandatory waiting periods. In addition to these administrative hurdles, probate is a public process. Once your estate enters probate, the details of what you owned, what you owed, and to whom you made your bequests are available to anyone who chooses to look. While most of us spend our lives protecting our privacy, probate proceedings can expose personal financial information to the public record. Anyone can walk into the county records office and review the inventory of your assets, your debts, and the final distributions of your estate. Privacy, once carefully guarded during life, can easily be lost in death if proper planning is not done.

It is important to understand that even if you have beneficiaries designated on your financial accounts, such as bank accounts, IRAs and brokerage accounts, real property including a home, vacation property, or rental real estate that is titled solely in your name will almost certainly be subject to probate proceedings. These assets must go through the court process before they can be legally transferred to your heirs. Similarly, financial accounts without designated beneficiaries may also require probate in order to transfer ownership. And, again, the probate process can be time-consuming, public, costly, and emotionally burdensome for your loved ones, adding stress and delays at an already difficult time.

WHY PROBATE OFTEN ISN'T AN ISSUE WHEN THE FIRST SPOUSE PASSES

If you've lost a spouse and didn't have to deal with probate, you're not alone. In many marriages, settling an estate after the first spouse's death is relatively straightforward and often involves little or no court involvement.

That's because many assets owned by married couples are structured to pass automatically to the surviving spouse. Homes held jointly, retirement accounts with named beneficiaries, life insurance policies, and accounts with transfer-on-death designations typically move directly to the surviving spouse by operation of law. When assets transfer this way, probate is often unnecessary.

For this reason, the death of the first spouse is frequently a non-event from a probate perspective. The surviving spouse may experience emotional and logistical challenges, but not the legal headaches often associated with probate.

There are exceptions. In second marriages, blended families, or situations where assets were intentionally structured through trusts, probate or trust administration may still come into play. But for many couples, estate planning issues do not fully surface until later, when the surviving spouse begins to think about what happens next.

That's why it's common for probate to feel like a distant concern—until it isn't. The real estate planning decisions often become more relevant after the first loss, when the focus shifts from transferring assets between spouses to ensuring they pass smoothly to the next generation.

THE BENEFITS OF A LIVING TRUST

For many people, especially those with real estate or significant assets, a properly structured living trust is often a better foundation for an estate plan. Even though only about 13% report having a living trust, according to a 2025 estate planning survey by Caring.com, upon your death, the assets held in your trust pass directly to your beneficiaries, without the need for probate. A trust remains private, avoids unnecessary court involvement, and can considerably speed up the process of settling your estate.

In fact, in a properly constructed estate plan, the living trust—not the will—serves as the central organizing document. A living trust is a separate legal entity, and when set up correctly, assets are removed from your personal name and retitled in the name of the trust. Although the trust becomes the formal owner, you, as the grantor and trustee during your lifetime, retain full authority over the assets it holds. You can continue to control, sell, borrow against, transfer, or otherwise manage the trust assets just as freely as you did when they were titled under your name. For tax purposes, the trust is reported under your Social Security number while you are alive, which often makes it feel like nothing has changed in your day-to-day financial life. From a practical standpoint, very little does change. But legally, you are building a structure that ensures a smooth and efficient transition of control should you become incapacitated or pass away.

The critical distinction arises upon your death. When everything is owned by the trust, nothing is technically held in your personal name so there is nothing to pass through probate. The trust, as a legal entity, does not "die." Instead, it becomes *irrevocable*, which means its terms can no longer be changed and it becomes a separate entity, which is why the trust must obtain its own tax identification number, and your named successor trustee steps in to follow the instructions you laid out, including managing the trust property, distributing assets to beneficiaries, and ultimately dissolving the trust when its terms have been fulfilled. This continuity is one of the greatest advantages of a properly funded living trust. It allows your affairs to be handled privately, efficiently, and according to your wishes without court interference. In the same way a corporation continues on after its founder dies, a living trust has its own legal life beyond you.

Importantly, the living trust also provides protection in the event of your incapacity. If you become unable to manage your own affairs, the successor trustee you named can step in immediately to manage the assets titled in the name of the trust, without court intervention, guardianship proceedings, or unnecessary delays. Because the trust owns the assets, and the trust terms specifically authorize the successor trustee to act, management of your financial life can continue seamlessly even if you are unable to give instructions yourself.

However, it is critical to understand that the protection and efficiency a trust provides only extends to the assets properly titled under its name. If you inadvertently leave assets outside of your trust, such as real estate held individually, or accounts titled solely in your name without beneficiary designations, those assets are not automatically protected by the trust terms. Instead, they are governed by the title ownership and by state law. For example, if you hold a joint bank account with rights of survivorship with someone, joint ownership law dictates that the surviving account holder receives the balance of that account outright upon your death, regardless of what your trust says. That account would not pass through the trust upon your death. Similarly, individually owned property without a beneficiary designation or trust titling would require probate to transfer, and the terms of your trust would not apply unless additional legal steps were taken.

To address the reality that assets may inadvertently be left out of the trust despite careful planning, a properly structured estate plan typically includes a "pour-over will." A pour-over will acts as a legal backstop, instructing that any assets not titled in the trust at your death be transferred into the trust through the probate process. While this still subjects those omitted assets to probate, it ensures that once probate concludes, the trust ultimately governs the distribution according to your original intentions. The pour-over will, while essential, is not a substitute for proper trust funding. Instead, it is a safety net to at least ensure your assets will pass to your selected beneficiaries. However, to minimize the need for probate and avoid unintended consequences, it is critical to title any new accounts or newly acquired property, such as real estate, raw land, expensive automobiles, RVs, or boats, in the name of your trust as soon as they are purchased.

When it comes to retirement accounts such as IRAs, 401(k)s, 403(b)s, and similar plans, the rules differ slightly. These accounts are not typically retitled into a trust during your lifetime because they are individually owned and protected under specific tax laws. IRAs, for example, are *Individual Retirement Accounts,* and cannot be titled in a trust or in the name of any other individual other than the original owner. In that case, you will designate beneficiaries directly on the account. In some cases, you may name individual beneficiaries; in other cases, the trust can be named as the beneficiary if doing so aligns with your broader estate planning goals. Either way, because retirement accounts pass to heirs by beneficiary designation rather than by will or trust, they do not go through probate if properly arranged. (If you neglect to designate a beneficiary or if your beneficiaries are deceased, your retirement accounts, life insurance policy, annuity, etc. could still be subject to probate.)

However, it is important to understand that while beneficiary designations determine what happens to retirement accounts at death, they do not provide protection during your lifetime. If you become incapacitated, your retirement accounts do not automatically fall under the control of your successor trustee. Instead, management authority would come through your financial power of attorney. Since the account is not owned by your trust, retirement accounts and the like would not be governed by the trust during your lifetime. Assets that name the trust as beneficiary become subject to the trust's terms only after your death. That means your financial power of attorney would need to be invoked for those accounts not titled under your trust in order to allow another person to manage or access those accounts on your behalf.

This is why a comprehensive estate plan does not rely solely on a trust or a will. It must include coordinated documents. This typically includes a living trust, a pour-over will, durable powers of attorney for financial management, and advance healthcare directives. Each document plays a critical role in protecting you, your wishes, and your assets. Estate planning is not just about death, but can also help during life, when clear, accessible authority can make all the difference.

Building a strong estate plan is not about predicting every future event. It is about creating a durable, integrated system that supports you through all phases of life—in health, incapacity, and eventually, the orderly transition of your legacy.

Updating Your Living Trust

As you may have concluded, updating your will after the death of a spouse is essential, but it should also prompt a broader review of your entire estate plan. This is the moment to ask, *is your plan structured to protect you—not just legally, but practically? Will it ensure your wishes are carried out efficiently and spare your loved ones from unnecessary legal burdens when they are already coping with loss?*

Few estate planning tools are as powerful as the living trust, and yet as misunderstood. While wills and trusts both play important roles, they are not interchangeable. As explained, a will alone cannot keep your estate out of probate. Only a properly structured and fully funded trust can do that.

If you and your spouse previously created a joint living trust, now is the time to revisit it carefully. After your spouse's passing, the trust likely needs to be revised, or in some cases divided, depending on how it was originally structured. Many married couples establish joint living trusts to streamline ownership and management of their assets during life, but after one spouse dies the trust's structure must adapt to your new situation.

One of the first questions to address is your role as the surviving spouse. If your trust contained what are often called "AB" provisions, which are generally created to minimize estate taxes, then the trust must now be divided into two separate parts: a survivor's trust (your portion) and a decedent's trust (your spouse's portion). The survivor's trust remains revocable and fully under your control, allowing you to amend, modify, or revoke it as needed. The decedent's trust, however, becomes irrevocable upon your spouse's death and must be administered according to the original terms outlined in the trust document. This structure, while once critical for federal estate tax efficiency, can be complex and often requires the guidance of an experienced estate attorney to administer properly. Managing two trusts brings new responsibilities and headaches though, like accounting separately for assets, filing distinct tax returns, maintaining required records, and ensuring compliance with both the trust terms and applicable state and federal laws.

Therefore, if you are not legally required to divide the trust, it may make more sense for you to create a new, single revocable living trust in your own name. If the prior tax-driven structures are no longer necessary, particularly in today's world where we've seen significant increases to federal estate tax exemption limits, you may prefer to consolidate your planning into a simpler, more streamlined trust. A single trust can clearly outline who will receive your assets, under what terms, and in what manner. It also allows you to maintain full control during your lifetime, avoid probate at death, and create flexibility for your beneficiaries. Simplifying the structure now can make future administration easier both for you and for those who will eventually settle your estate.

However, moving to a new, single trust is not always the best choice. In some cases, maintaining the original division between a survivor's trust and a decedent's trust may still be important to protect the interests of other beneficiaries. For example, if you and your spouse had children from previous marriages, such as a blended family situation, the original trust may have been designed specifically to ensure that certain assets pass to your spouse's children separately from your own. Consolidating into a single new trust could unintentionally override those original protections, potentially leading to family conflict or even legal disputes after your death.

Another example is if the decedent's trust holds assets meant to be preserved for future generations, such as specific gifts to grandchildren or charitable bequests. In that case, the trust's irrevocable terms protect those assets from being spent, given away, or otherwise redirected during your lifetime. Simplifying the structure by creating a new trust could expose those previously protected assets to new risks, whether through remarriage, creditors, or changing priorities over time.

Finally, if creditor protection or remarriage protection was built into the original estate plan through the irrevocable decedent's trust, creating a new, fully revocable trust could unintentionally eliminate those safeguards. A decedent's trust typically shelters its assets from new claims, while a fully revocable trust remains accessible and vulnerable as long as you are alive.

In short, while simplifying your estate plan can offer clarity and ease of administration, it should only be considered when it truly aligns with your family structure, your financial goals, and your legacy intentions. Before consolidating trusts, it's important to carefully review the original trust terms, assess your current situation, and consult with qualified legal counsel to be sure no unintended consequences could arise.

Irrevocable Trusts

Beyond revising your living trust, now may also be the time to consider whether new irrevocable trusts should be part of your updated estate strategy. Irrevocable trusts can serve important roles in asset protection, Medicaid planning, charitable giving, or transferring wealth to future generations in a tax-advantaged way. For example, if you anticipate significant long-term care needs, setting up an irrevocable Medicaid asset protection trust early can help shield assets while preserving eligibility for benefits later. Irrevocable trusts are powerful tools but come with notable trade-offs. Once assets are transferred into an irrevocable trust, you typically relinquish personal control over them. Decisions about creating new irrevocable structures should always be made thoughtfully and with professional legal and tax advice.

As you can see, there is much to consider, and every situation is unique. A truly effective estate plan often requires a customized approach. That is why having the right advisors by your side matters. You need professionals who understand both the technical and personal aspects of estate planning. That can make all the difference.

Funding Your Trust—What Goes In, What Stays Out and What Is Often Overlooked

Once you establish the appropriate structure, the next and equally important step is to properly fund the trust. Every asset you intend to be governed by your trust must be retitled into the trust's name. This includes bank accounts, investment accounts, real estate, business interests, and valuable personal property.

Funding is not a one-time administrative task. It is the operational step that gives your trust its true power and it must be maintained over time. Without proper and ongoing funding, even the most perfectly drafted trust can fail to avoid probate, delay distributions, or undermine the very protections you worked so hard to put in place.

If you open a new bank account, purchase real estate, refinance a property, invest in a brokerage account, or acquire valuable personal property like vehicles, boats, or collectibles pay close attention to how assets are titled. If new assets are not properly titled in the name of your trust, they may fall outside its protection and inadvertently create gaps that force your estate back through probate.

Continuous attention to funding is what transforms a trust from a theoretical plan into a fully functioning legal structure. Every time your financial situation changes, whether through new purchases, asset sales, inheritances, business interests, or major gifts, it is important to revisit your trust funding. Proper maintenance ensures that your estate plan remains complete, integrated, and ready to serve you and your loved ones exactly as intended when needed.

Although proper funding of your trust is essential, it's important to understand that not every asset necessarily needs to be placed into your trust. In some cases, certain assets can be left outside of the trust intentionally, especially when dealing with what are known as "small estates." Many states offer simplified probate procedures for estates under a certain dollar value, allowing smaller amounts of assets to transfer to heirs without the full probate process. These limits vary by state but are often generous enough to accommodate personal belongings, modest bank accounts, or other small assets without imposing significant legal hurdles.

For example, if you leave a personal checking account with only a few thousand dollars outside of your trust, your heirs may be able to transfer those funds using an affidavit procedure, rather than going through formal probate. Similarly, household furnishings, personal effects, or day-to-day vehicles are often excluded from trust funding unless they carry unusually high values.

Leaving minor or practical assets outside the trust can simplify your life without jeopardizing your overall estate plan. However, this strategy must be used carefully and deliberately. If assets outside the trust exceed your state's small estate threshold, they could trigger probate, even if the bulk of your estate is properly protected. Likewise, if you leave out significant assets, such as real estate, major investment accounts, or business interests, you risk undermining the very protections your trust was designed to provide.

Accounts with designated beneficiaries, such as IRAs, typically cannot be titled in the name of your trust as already noted; however, you may choose to name your trust as the beneficiary, depending on your overall estate planning goals. For other types of accounts, particularly bank or brokerage accounts with large balances, you generally can title the account in the name of your trust. In those cases, it's often preferable to do so rather than relying on a transfer-on-death (TOD) designation. Titling the account in your trust allows the assets to flow seamlessly according to the terms you've laid out in the trust, without relying on beneficiary arrangements, unless you intentionally want to leave that account outside the trust for a specific reason.

It's often much simpler and safer to streamline your estate plan by ensuring that all eligible assets flow through your trust. Relying on a patchwork of beneficiary designations can become burdensome, especially if you move, change banks, or open new accounts. In those transitions, it's easy to overlook a beneficiary update or miss designating one altogether. I've seen far too many cases where a single missed designation caused unnecessary probate complications, despite the individual's best intentions.

Per Stirpes or Per Capita

The legal world still leans on old Latin phrases. You see them sprinkled across contracts and estate forms, and two important ones for estate planning are per stirpes and per capita. They may sound foreign, but they carry very real consequences for how your money is passed on.

When you designate a beneficiary on your 401(k) or IRA, or add a TOD to your bank account, it might sound simple. *I want my children to receive an equal share*. But what is not addressed is what happens if one of your children predeceases you. Should the account be divided among the survivors, or should their share pass down to their children and through their family branch?

That's the difference between per stirpes and per capita. Per stirpes passes the share down the family line, keeping that branch of the family included. Per capita simply splits the account among the surviving beneficiaries at the same level, cutting off the line of the one who passed. Of course, if your children are unmarried and without children, that might be exactly what you want. But when there are grandchildren or even great grandchildren, the considerations might be more complex.

Neither approach is right or wrong, of course. It depends on your wishes, but the critical point is that many financial institutions set the rule for you. Some only honor one method. Others define the terms differently than you might assume. For instance, one brokerage firm may only allow a per stirpes designation but limit how far down the family tree it extends. Another may only allow per capita, meaning grandchildren are excluded entirely unless you list them by name. Some institutions create their own version of "per stirpes" in the fine print that doesn't match the traditional legal definition. Custodians, such as banks, brokerages, and retirement plan administrators can adapt or even redefine these terms in their own paperwork, and it is their version that ultimately controls how your account is distributed. These differences can lead to very different outcomes for your family depending on where your accounts are held.

This is where a trust restores control. Instead of being bound by a custodian's default policy, you decide exactly how your legacy will be divided. A trust ensures that your wishes, not an institution's paperwork, determine the outcome. If you want your assets divided only among the surviving beneficiaries at the same level, you can set it up that way. If you want future grandchildren included and protected, you can build that in as well.

ANNUITIES AND LIFE INSURANCE

Be careful with annuities and life insurance. While they can be integrated with your trust, the mechanics and implications differ.

In many cases it may be best to name your trust as the beneficiary but not the owner. Life insurance is often easiest to coordinate this way, allowing the death benefit to flow according to your trust's instructions, which is useful when you want to stagger distributions, protect heirs, or align with other estate planning goals. In some cases the trust can also be named as the owner, though this adds complexity and should be done only with legal guidance to preserve potential tax benefits.

Annuities, on the other hand, are even more sensitive to trust involvement. While a trust can be named as owner or beneficiary, doing so may limit tax deferral or trigger faster distribution after death, resulting in accelerated taxation. These are not one-size-fits-all decisions and should be reviewed carefully with your advisors to ensure they support your broader objectives.

Ultimately, decisions about what to fund and what to leave outside the trust should be made thoughtfully, ideally with guidance from your attorney and financial advisor, along with any other advisors you may lean on. A properly crafted plan strikes a balance between comprehensive protection and practical flexibility, ensuring that everything important is covered while allowing for the realities of day-to-day living.

SMALL ESTATES

Not all estates are subject to probate. As already noted, every state offers a simplified process, typically what's known as a "small estate." If the total value of assets falls below a certain threshold (which varies by state), heirs may be able to transfer property using a small estate affidavit or similar procedure, avoiding the time and cost of formal probate. This can be especially helpful when dealing with modest estates or when only a few assets were left outside the trust due to oversight.

On the next page is a list of small estate affidavit limits for all 50 US states as of 2026. These thresholds determine whether an estate qualifies for simplified probate procedures, allowing heirs to transfer assets without undergoing formal probate. Please note that these limits can vary based on specific circumstances and may be subject to change; consequently, it's advisable to consult local statutes or with legal professionals for the most current information. This list is intended as a general guide and may not reflect the exact requirements in your state.

NOTE: Some states have varying limits based on specific conditions, such as the type of property or the relationship of the heir to the decedent. For instance, Maryland's limit ranges from $50,000 to $100,000 depending on the circumstances. Nevada's limit varies between $25,000 and $100,000 based on the nature of the assets. While this list provides a general overview of small estate limits as of 2026, each state's procedures, thresholds, and requirements can vary and are subject to change. For more detailed information about your specific state's small estate process, consult your state's probate code, court resources, or a qualified estate attorney in your area.

I understand that the details of estate planning can feel overwhelming, especially for those newly widowed. If your spouse previously handled much of the family's financial management, the process can feel even more burdensome. But taking the time now to properly update or establish your trust is one of the strongest ways you can protect yourself, simplify your future, and honor the legacy you and your spouse built together. An estate plan is not just a bunch of legal documents. As you have learned, it is a living plan, a framework if you will for preserving, protecting, and ultimately passing on the assets you have worked so hard to build to the people who matter most.

State	Small Estate Limit	State	Small Estate Limit
Alabama	$25,000	Montana	$50,000
Alaska	$150,000	Nebraska	$50,000
Arizona	$75,000	Nevada	$25,000-$100,000
Arkansas	$100,000	New Hampshire	$10,000
California	$208,850	New Jersey	$50,000
Colorado	$66,000	New Mexico	$50,000
Connecticut	$40,000	New York	$30,000
Delaware	$30,000	North Carolina	$30,000
D.C.	$40,000	North Dakota	$50,000
Florida	$75,000	Ohio	$100,000
Georgia	$10,000	Oklahoma	$50,000
Hawaii	$100,000	Oregon	$275,000
Idaho	$100,000	Pennsylvania	$50,000
Illinois	$150,000	Rhode Island	$15,000
Indiana	$50,000	South Carolina	$25,000
Iowa	$100,000	South Dakota	$50,000
Kansas	$40,000	Tennessee	$25,000
Kentucky	$15,000	Texas	$75,000
Louisiana	$75,000	Utah	$100,000
Maine	$20,000	Vermont	$10,000
Maryland	$50,000-$100,000	Virginia	$50,000
Massachusetts	$25,000	Washington	$100,000
Michigan	$21,000	West Virginia	$100,000
Minnesota	$50,000	Wisconsin	$50,000
Mississippi	$50,000	Wyoming	$200,000
Missouri	$40,000		

POWERS OF ATTORNEY: NAMING SOMEONE WHO CAN ACT IF YOU CANNOT

One of the most important practical gaps to address is your power of attorney. In most cases, your spouse was likely the person you designated to act on your behalf if you became unable to manage your financial affairs. Now that they are no longer available, that protection no longer exists. Without updating it you are vulnerable to unnecessary legal complications if something happens to you.

A financial power of attorney (POA) is a key document that authorizes someone you trust to manage your financial matters if you are unable to act. This authority can include paying your bills, accessing and managing your bank and brokerage accounts, handling real estate transactions, managing retirement distributions, signing legal documents, and ensuring that your financial life continues smoothly if you become incapacitated. Without a valid and up-to-date POA, your loved ones might be forced to go to court to establish a guardianship or conservatorship just to manage your everyday affairs, which is a costly, time-consuming, and public process that easily could have been avoided.

While your living trust provides instructions for managing and distributing the assets held inside the trust, a financial power of attorney plays a different but equally important role. The POA governs your financial matters *outside of the trust.* This includes assets that may not be titled in the trust, such as retirement accounts, certain personal property, insurance claims, government benefits, and financial accounts that were either intentionally or unintentionally left outside the trust.

Together the living trust and the financial power of attorney form a comprehensive safety net. The trustee manages trust assets, while the agent under your POA manages non-trust assets.

Without both documents properly in place, gaps in authority can arise, leaving your loved ones scrambling to petition the court for permission to act at precisely the time when private, timely action is most needed.

In many cases you may choose to name the same person to serve both roles. In fact having a single, trusted individual serve as both your successor trustee and your agent under a power of attorney can simplify matters and reduce confusion. However, you are not required to appoint the same person for both roles. You may select different individuals based on their specific strengths, availability, or expertise. What matters most is ensuring that the people you choose are trustworthy, capable, and fully understand the responsibilities they may someday need to assume.

When revisiting or creating a new POA, one of the first decisions you must make is what type of power you want to grant. A durable power of attorney becomes effective immediately upon signing and remains valid even if you become incapacitated later. A springing power of attorney, on the other hand, only becomes effective once a doctor or court formally declares you incapacitated. While a springing POA might sound appealing to those who worry about handing over power too early, it can create practical problems. Institutions like banks, investment firms, and title companies may refuse to honor a springing POA until specific legal proof of incapacity is presented. Delays at critical moments could prevent timely bill payments, asset management, or needed care decisions. In most cases, particularly for widowed individuals, a durable power of attorney is the preferred choice because it ensures there is no disruption or delay in the event of a sudden health event. However, because this authority can be broad and immediate, it's essential to choose someone you trust implicitly and to consider safeguards to prevent potential abuse.

Another important aspect is naming successor agents. Life happens, and the person you name today may not be able or willing to serve when the time comes. Always name at least one backup. Again, it should go without saying that this ought to be people you trust implicitly. You will want to put forth every effort possible to ensure that your financial affairs are protected no matter what happens. Successor agents provide vital continuity and avoid the risk of being left unprotected if your first choice declines or is unavailable.

I'm reminded of Lenny, who had named his wife as his financial power of attorney, but hadn't named a backup. Updating the document was something he intended to do, but like many people he never got around to it. After his wife passed away he delayed updating his estate plan, including his POA, despite my encouragement. Having no children, Lenny felt unsure about whom to appoint, so he put off the decision.

A few years later, sadly, Lenny suffered a severe stroke. His extended family came in from out of state to help, but when they contacted his bank to pay urgent bills and manage his accounts, they were told they had no legal authority. Without a valid POA on file, and with no successor named, Lenny's cousin had to petition the court for conservatorship, which was a public, expensive, and time-consuming process. It was even more challenging because his cousin didn't live nearby and had to navigate court proceedings long distance. It took nearly four months before he was granted the legal authority needed to manage Lenny's non-trust assets. That could have meant four months of unpaid bills, frozen accounts, and significant financial strain. Fortunately, Lenny had also funded his living trust properly, which allowed his successor trustee to access trust assets in the interim to cover urgent needs. But the struggle and the heavy burden on his out-of-state family could have been entirely avoided with one updated document.

Choosing the right person to serve as your financial power of attorney, or your trustee for that matter, is one of the most important decisions you will make in your estate planning process. This individual will have access to your financial life including your accounts, your assets, and your responsibilities, including the potential need to make significant decisions on your behalf during times of incapacity or, in the case of a trustee, upon your death. Clearly trustworthiness, competence, and availability are key.

In most cases, the best approach is to name a single primary agent—someone you trust to act decisively and responsibly—and then name one or two successor agents who can step in if the first person is unable or unwilling to serve. If you have adult children, it can be tempting to name all of them together as co-agents to avoid feelings of favoritism. However, appointing multiple people to act jointly can create unintended complications. Banks, brokerage firms, and other institutions often require all co-agents to sign for every transaction, which can cause delays, especially if one person is unavailable. It can also lead to disagreements among your children at a time when clear, unified action is needed. Choosing one person avoids confusion, streamlines decision-making, and reduces the risk of conflict among your loved ones. If you feel strongly about involving multiple children, you can build in communication requirements or advisory roles without requiring unanimous signatures for every financial action.

But what if you do not have children, or you do not have someone you feel comfortable appointing? This is more common than many may realize, but there are solutions. You might consider a trusted relative, a close friend, or even a professional fiduciary. You can choose a licensed individual or corporate entity whose job is to act as a neutral, responsible agent on your behalf.

For estates under $5 million, corporate trustee services offered by banks and large trust companies may not be practical or even available, as many require higher minimum asset levels and tend to offer standardized, institutional service. In these situations appointing a trusted individual, such as a family member or close friend, as trustee can be a reasonable and cost-effective option, especially when paired with professional guidance from a financial advisor, CPA, or estate attorney. Another alternative is to work with a licensed private fiduciary, where available, who can serve in a professional trustee or power of attorney role for a fee. This approach can offer a more personal and flexible experience than larger institutions. Some attorneys offer fiduciary services, subject to minimum estate sizes. In some cases, families use a collaborative model, where the named individual trustee retains outside professionals and continues to use their existing investment custodian to manage the trust assets. Each of these options has tradeoffs, and it's important to choose a structure that aligns with your values, complexity of assets, and long-term goals.

No matter who you appoint, the key is to choose someone who will respect your wishes, understand the seriousness of the role, and have the competence to manage your financial affairs prudently. It is better to take the time now to select the right person thoughtfully than to leave your loved ones facing uncertainty or forced to go through the court system later. Many attorneys can help guide you to identify the best options for your situation.

Updating your financial power of attorney is a significant step toward protecting your independence. It's not just a paperwork exercise. It gives you the ability to appoint someone you trust to act when you cannot, and to ensure your financial life continues with minimal disruption. In widowhood, where you are now the sole steward of your future, this protection is more important than ever.

HEALTH CARE DIRECTIVES: ENSURING YOUR MEDICAL WISHES ARE RESPECTED

Updating your estate plan isn't just about finances. It's also about making sure your voice is heard when it comes to medical decisions, especially if you reach a point where you can no longer speak for yourself. In many ways, updating your health care directives is one of the most emotionally important steps you will take.

There are several key documents you will want to review or create. An Advanced Health Care Directive, sometimes called a Living Will, specifies what types of medical treatment you want, or do not want, if you are unable to communicate your wishes. This can include decisions about resuscitation, mechanical ventilation, artificial nutrition, pain management, and end-of-life care. Clear instructions help guide your loved ones and doctors if difficult choices must be made.

You will also need to update your Health Care Power of Attorney (also known as a Health Care Proxy). This document names the person you trust to make medical decisions for you if you are unable to make them yourself. If you had previously named your spouse, that authority is now void and you will need to designate someone new. Choosing a health care agent is, obviously, deeply personal. It's not just about who you trust, it's about who has the emotional strength to carry out your wishes under pressure, even if others disagree or emotions are running high.

In addition, you should execute a HIPAA Authorization. This document allows your health care agent to access your medical records and speak freely with your providers. Without it, your agent may run into roadblocks when trying to get critical information needed to make decisions on your behalf.

If you have multiple adult children, it's not unusual to divide responsibilities based on their strengths. You might name one child as your financial power of attorney and another as your health care agent. Some individuals are more comfortable handling medical decisions, while others may be better suited to managing financial affairs. Choosing separate agents can also reduce family tension by giving each child a clear and distinct role. However, coordination between the two is still important, especially when health care decisions may have financial implications, such as long-term care arrangements or major treatment expenses.

Ultimately, what matters most is that the person (or people) you name are willing and able to honor your values and wishes, not their own, and can act decisively under stressful circumstances. This is not a popularity contest or a question of birth order. It's about choosing advocates who understand you, respect you, and can represent your interests clearly when it matters most.

Taking the time now to update these documents, and to have open, honest conversations with those you appoint can relieve your loved ones of enormous emotional burdens later. It ensures that the decisions made on your behalf reflect your choices, not someone else's guesswork.

BENEFICIARIES AND OWNERSHIP: WHAT NEEDS TO BE RETITLED OR REVIEWED?

As already explained, many assets pass *outside* of your will or trust directly through beneficiary designations you made with banks, insurance companies, or retirement plan providers. These designations override what's in your estate documents, meaning if they aren't updated, your assets could unintentionally go to the wrong person. It's essential to review and update your beneficiaries directly with each institution for assets like:

- life insurance policies
- retirement accounts (IRAs, 401(k)s, Roths)
- annuities
- transfer-on-death (TOD) or Payable-on-death (POD) accounts

Ownership of other assets must also be reviewed carefully. If you jointly owned property or accounts with your spouse, you may need to retitle them in your name alone. This includes real estate, joint bank accounts, and investment accounts. Not addressing ownership changes can lead to unexpected complications later, such as probate issues, frozen accounts, or unintended beneficiaries.

This is why updating your living trust is not enough on its own. Beneficiary designations and titling decisions are equally important to ensuring your wishes are honored. Think of your estate plan as the blueprint, and your beneficiary forms and asset titles as the actual construction. They must match.

TRANSFER-ON-DEATH (TOD) DESIGNATIONS

TODs have become an increasingly popular estate planning tool, especially for individuals with simpler financial lives and smaller estates. In many cases, they offer a streamlined and low-cost way to pass assets like bank accounts, brokerage accounts, vehicles, and even real estate directly to named beneficiaries. Like a living trust, a TOD designation allows those assets to bypass probate, providing privacy and efficiency. For someone who is single, has one or two adult beneficiaries, and minimal complexity in their estate, a TOD can be good enough, particularly when the goal is simply to ensure the smooth transfer of assets without legal entanglements.

But for all their simplicity, TODs come with limitations that make them inadequate for more comprehensive planning. They provide no control over how or when assets are distributed. For instance, beneficiaries receive their inheritance outright, regardless of age, financial maturity, or other circumstances. TODs also lack backup planning. If a named beneficiary predeceases the account holder and no alternate is listed, the asset may still end up in probate. And how the assets pass down the family branch, as described above with per stirpes or per capita, can matter. Further, each asset must be individually titled with TOD instructions, resulting in a piecemeal approach that lacks the cohesion of a centralized living trust.

TODs also fail to address incapacity. They offer no provisions for managing assets during life if the owner becomes unable to do so. And while neither TODs nor standard living trusts offer outright protection from estate taxes or creditors, a trust can be designed with far more flexibility for multigenerational planning, blended families, spendthrift heirs, and disability planning. For those with more complex goals, greater assets, or simply the desire to retain control beyond death, a revocable living trust remains the superior planning tool.

A Word of Caution about Beneficiary Designations

I've found that some attorneys or financial professionals, oddly enough, suggest that simply naming your trust as the beneficiary on accounts is "good enough" implying you don't need to fund the trust directly. But this approach can lead to serious problems. Beneficiary designations are powerful tools for passing assets efficiently, yet they are not a substitute for ensuring your trust is properly funded and able to function as designed. When you rely solely on beneficiary designations, you risk bypassing the trust entirely for key assets, undermining your ability to coordinate your wishes across your estate.

It's also easy to miss a beneficiary update when opening a new account, moving assets, or making financial changes during stressful life events. That oversight can cause an account to default to probate, despite your intentions. This can also create inconsistencies, where some assets follow the trust's instructions and others do not, resulting in confusion, conflict, or unintended outcomes. Even worse, beneficiary designations only apply after death. They offer no help if you become incapacitated during your lifetime, when the trust is meant to step in and protect you. And for assets like real estate, failing to retitle them into the trust may still expose them to probate. Some states now permit TOD arrangements for real estate, but that still is not a substitute for a well-structured estate plan.

Beneficiary designations and trust funding must work together. They don't replace each other. Keep in mind that your estate plan is only as strong as the coordination between your documents, your beneficiary forms, and how your assets are titled. It's not enough to create a well-thought-out trust on paper. Your plan must be fully aligned in practice to deliver the protection, efficiency, and peace of mind you intended.

Some attorneys see TODs and POAs as a simpler, lower-cost workaround. But from a planning perspective, that patchwork approach doesn't give you the consistency and protection that comes with properly funding your trust outright. A well-funded trust acts as the hub of your estate, coordinating everything in one place rather than scattering the rules across multiple institutions' forms.

We have a client who has two disabled adult children. Imagine my shock when they told me their attorney had advised them a will was sufficient. The plan, they were told, was that after their deaths, their assets would "pour over" into the trust as written into their will, and eventually fund a special needs trust that had been drafted for their children. On paper it sounded neat and clean, but in reality, it was full of risks and unnecessary headaches.

A special needs trust is often created to protect a child or grandchild with a disability, ensuring they receive care and support without losing eligibility for government benefits such as Medicaid or Supplemental Security Income (SSI). The way this trust is created matters. If the special needs trust is written into your living trust, it springs into action immediately at your death. The successor trustee can step in, manage the assets, and provide for your loved one seamlessly, all without court involvement. It's private, efficient, and ensures continuity of care.

If, instead, the special needs trust is set up through your will, it doesn't exist until after probate is complete. That means a delay, sometimes a long one, before the trust is funded and able to support your loved one. During that time, the court process controls everything, and your family may be left scrambling to cover expenses. Even once probate ends, the assets may remain subject to court oversight, annual accountings, or restrictions that add cost and complexity.

The difference is night and day. A living trust with a built-in special needs provision provides speed, privacy, and stability, while a will-based approach introduces delay, red tape, and uncertainty. For a child or grandchild who depends on that support, the choice isn't just about avoiding probate, it's about ensuring their well-being without disruption.

I've run across other situations where clients were told by their legal counsel not to fund their trust until they passed away. While I'm not an attorney, I don't agree with that logic. Waiting defeats the very purpose of a living trust. A trust is designed to step in immediately, not only at death but also if you become incapacitated, ensuring someone you trust can manage your affairs without court involvement. I've seen firsthand how much more smoothly estates settle when the trust is already funded and ready to function.

I've also met families who were advised to use Transfer on Death (TOD) designations for their entire estate, even for real estate. Again, I disagree. TODs can be useful in limited circumstances, but they do nothing during your lifetime if you become unable to manage your own affairs, and they don't provide the same level of coordination and protection that a trust offers. Relying solely on TODs can create gaps, inconsistencies, and unintended consequences, exactly the kind of problems a well-structured trust is meant to prevent.

The protections provided by a trust are during your lifetime, not just after death. If an accident, illness, or cognitive decline occurs, having assets already titled in the trust allows a successor trustee to manage them privately and efficiently without needing court involvement, and without the risk that a POA may be rejected.

In addition, funding the trust during life opens the door to more advanced planning opportunities. For example, certain trusts allow for strategic gifting during your lifetime, which can help manage estate taxes, protect assets from long-term care risks, and better position the family for future transitions. In some cases, proactive planning inside the trust can help shield assets from being depleted by medical or custodial care expenses, while still preserving flexibility and control. Of course, these strategies can be complex, and it's important to work closely with qualified legal, tax, and financial advisors to ensure they are aligned with your overall goals and circumstances.

The bottom line is trusts and estate planning documents are powerful tools, but they are only as effective as the care taken to align them properly with the assets they are designed to protect.

Funding is not just about transferring ownership. It is about activating the protections the trust was built to provide. After all, a trust is not just about what happens after you are gone. It's about ensuring there is a clear, private, efficient path forward during every stage of life. Funding your trust while you are alive is not an optional step in my view. It's essential to making the entire plan work the way you intended. Creating the right documents is only half the equation. Funding the trust properly ensures that those documents actually work when they are needed most.

SHOULD SOMETHING HAPPEN: THE PERSONAL DETAILS THAT COMPLETE THE PLAN

Unfortunately, not everything that matters fits neatly into a legal document. Wills and trusts are necessary, but they don't capture the personal, everyday information that makes life work behind the scenes. That's where your personal organizer, something we call "Should Something Happen," comes into the picture. It's not a legal document, but it is one of the most powerful gifts you can leave behind for the people who will one day step in to help.

A complete organizer serves as the bridge between your formal estate plan and the practical realities your loved ones will face. It gathers in one place all the critical information, instructions, and preferences that can otherwise cause confusion, delays, or heartache during an already difficult time. Your organizer might include a list of important passwords and digital account instructions, a directory of key contacts such as your financial advisor, CPA, attorney, insurance agent, and primary physician, and notes about pet care, guardianship wishes, or even favorite routines and food preferences for your pets. It should also record where to find important documents such as vehicle titles, property deeds, mortgage and loan information, insurance policies, and safe deposit box keys or storage unit access instructions. You might also include funeral or memorial preferences, formal arrangements, personal wishes, and important cultural or religious traditions you want honored. Some people choose to add a personal letter to loved ones, sharing values, reflections, hopes, and encouragement for the future.

A thoughtfully prepared organizer saves time, reduces stress, and helps ensure that even the smallest but most meaningful details are not overlooked. It is a final act of love, practicality, and respect for those you care about most. Whether you call it a "Should Something Happen" binder, a "Financial Organizer," or simply your personal roadmap, what matters most is that it exists and that the right people know where to find it when the time comes.

If you don't have a personal organizer yet, or if you're not sure where to start, you can find a downloadable copy of the template we use with our clients in the resources section. It's designed to help you gather everything in one place, thoughtfully and thoroughly, so you can create a resource your loved ones will truly appreciate.

WHEN TO TACKLE THIS—AND WHY SOONER IS USUALLY BETTER

There's no perfect time to face all of this. Some people are ready within weeks of losing their spouse, but for others, it takes months or even longer to feel prepared to make these heavy decisions. What matters most is not when you start, but that you *do start,* and that you don't let uncertainty or discomfort delay action indefinitely.

Of course, waiting too long can create risks. Outdated documents can cause confusion or legal disputes among family members. Tax planning opportunities that could have preserved more of your estate may be missed forever simply because no action was taken in time. Unclear or undocumented intentions often lead to unnecessary conflict among those you hoped to protect, sometimes damaging relationships beyond repair. Perhaps most seriously, leaving major pieces unfinished can result in gaps in your legal protection, meaning that if something unexpected happens to you, the people you trust may have no clear authority to step in, and courts may need to intervene.

At the same time, it's important to remember that you don't have to do everything all at once. Trying to update your estate plan, change ownership titles, revise beneficiaries, organize personal records, and complete financial planning all in a single sprint is overwhelming for even the most motivated person. Instead, break the process into manageable steps. Create a checklist. Tackle one or two tasks at a time. Prioritize the most urgent gaps first, such as beneficiary designations and medical directives, then work your way through the rest methodically. Talk to your advisors. Ask questions when you're unsure. Take breaks when you need them. The key is to stay in motion, even if it's slow at times.

You have spent a lifetime building what you have. You've earned the right to protect it properly, and with care, intention, and dignity. Completing this work is not just about legal compliance. It is an act of love toward yourself and those you will one day leave behind. And like so many things in life, the earlier you start, the more choices you have, and the more peace of mind you can create for today, tomorrow, and for whatever the future may hold.

Updating Isn't Just Legal—It's Emotional

Much of the focus has been on legal updates, titling, forms, and structure. But the work is about much more than paperwork. It's about stepping into a life that has been permanently changed, and doing so with the strength to move forward, the hope to keep building, and the determination to live in a way that honors both what was and what still can be. You are still in charge. You still have the power to protect your values, preserve your wishes, and pass down not just your assets, but your principles, your lessons, and your hopes for the people you love. That is the real gift, and it is one that far outweighs any piece of paper or financial statement.

CHAPTER SIX

Death, Debt, and Taxes

Essential Steps to Safeguard What You Have

After the funeral: The financial realities no one warns you about.

Losing your spouse doesn't just change your emotional world, it reshapes your financial identity. Overnight, roles shift. Accounts that were once shared are now solely yours. Income may decline, while tax responsibilities rise. Even the financial decisions you once made together, sometimes without much thought, are now entirely your responsibility. Some changes are immediate and unmistakable, such as managing day-to-day bills or signing forms that once required two signatures. But others creep in more quietly, like a change in tax brackets, a smaller Social Security benefit, or the unsettling realization that some expenses don't shrink just because your household has.

Widowhood requires navigating practical and technical changes, including those tied to debt, credit and taxes. What happens to a credit card that was in your spouse's name? Are you liable for medical bills or personal loans they left behind? How should you handle a mortgage held jointly or one that wasn't? And what, exactly, is the "widow's penalty," and how can you prepare for its ripple effect on your long-term finances?

You don't need to become a tax strategist or estate attorney, but you do need a working knowledge of what to expect, what questions to ask, and where to turn for help. However, debt, death, and taxes have a way of complicating even the most straightforward financial lives, and widowhood reshapes the financial landscape ahead. Understanding how debt and taxes change after the loss of a spouse allows you to protect what you have, plan deliberately, and move forward with stability.

Let's start with debts. What happens when your spouse dies with credit card debt, car loans, or medical bills in their name? Are you liable for those debts? The rules vary depending on the type of account, how it was titled, and your state's laws. But one thing is certain, not all debt automatically becomes yours. Consequently, knowing where you are responsible and where you are not is the first step in protecting your estate and avoiding costly missteps.

WHAT HAPPENS TO CREDIT CARDS?

One of the first financial questions that often surfaces after the death of a spouse is what happens to their credit card debt. The answer depends on how the accounts were structured and, in some cases, where you live. If you were a joint account holder, you are legally responsible for the remaining balance, even if your spouse was the only one using the card. Joint credit cards carry shared liability, meaning both parties are equally obligated, regardless of who made the charges.

But if the credit card was in your spouse's name only, even if you were an authorized user, you are generally not responsible for the debt. In that case, the creditor must file a claim against your spouse's estate to seek repayment. If the estate lacks sufficient assets, the debt may go unpaid, and that's not your burden to carry. This remains true even in community property states, like California. While debts incurred during marriage are typically treated as shared, authorized user-only status does not create personal liability. Creditors may have limited rights to pursue repayment from community property assets, but they typically cannot demand payment from your separate assets or force you to cover a debt you never agreed to.

If there is no probate (because everything was held in trust, passed by beneficiary designation, or owned jointly) that limits what a creditor can access. Credit card companies are unsecured creditors, meaning they don't have a legal claim on specific assets like a home or vehicle. And if your spouse left no assets subject to probate, there may be nothing to collect from at all. Trusts and jointly titled accounts are not automatically exposed to creditor claims unless the trust assumes the debt or the surviving spouse voluntarily pays it. In many cases, the debt simply dies with the decedent.

Of course, that doesn't stop collectors from trying. Some will send letters or make calls that suggest you're responsible, even when you're not. Their goal is to collect, so they may try to confuse, intimidate, or even guilt you into paying. Don't let the tone or language or phone call override the facts. You have the right to request written validation of the debt, confirm your legal relationship to the account, and decline to pay if you are not liable. If there is no estate to pursue and you didn't sign for the debt, you're under no obligation.

It's also important to note that trusts and joint accounts are not automatically subject to creditor claims. Unless the trust specifically assumes the debt (which is rare), or unless the surviving spouse voluntarily pays it from trust assets, creditors are often left with no legal recourse. This is not about dodging responsibility. It's about understanding that the law distinguishes between personal and estate liability. If the estate doesn't exist, or the assets are protected by legal structure, the creditor has no standing.

While rare, creditors can petition the court under certain circumstances to seek payment from otherwise protected assets, so proper legal review is always recommended. If you're unsure about your responsibility, this is the time to seek professional guidance. A financial advisor, estate attorney, or consumer law specialist can help you understand your position and protect your assets. However, in most cases, the debt essentially dies with the person, unless you're legally responsible for it. The goal here isn't to "avoid" paying what you actually owe. Rather, it's to make sound decisions that preserve your financial health, especially during a time when every dollar counts.

WHAT ABOUT AUTO LOANS AND OTHER SECURED DEBT?

Unlike credit card balances, auto loans are secured debt and that means the loan is backed by collateral. In this case, the collateral is the vehicle itself. If the loan isn't paid, the lender has the legal right to repossess the car, sell it, and apply the proceeds toward the unpaid balance.

That changes how things are handled after the death of a spouse. If the car loan was in both of your names, or if you, as the surviving spouse, choose to keep and use the vehicle, then continuing the payments becomes part of the new financial reality. Most lenders will allow you to continue making payments or refinance the car loan in your own name, especially if you've been making payments all along. But they are not required to do so, and they may instead require proof of your ability to pay or ask you to complete a formal application to assume the debt.

If the loan was in your spouse's name only, and you are not a cosigner, the situation is more complex. The lender may repossess the vehicle if payments stop, even if the title transferred to you automatically through a trust or joint ownership. Of course, you can negotiate with the lender, which makes sense if you want to keep the vehicle, but you are not necessarily responsible for the loan unless you agree to take it on. Again, community property rules can complicate this, so state law matters. In California, for example, a car purchased during marriage is generally considered community property, and the loan attached to it may also be viewed as a community debt. However, this doesn't automatically mean you're personally on the hook. If you didn't cosign, the lender cannot force you to repay the debt from your separate assets unless you assume the loan or reaffirm it in your name.

This is the key difference with secured loans. The lender's power lies in the collateral. If payments continue, you keep the vehicle. If they stop, the lender can take the car. But they cannot sue you personally for the debt unless you're legally obligated on the loan. If the car is repossessed and sold for less than the outstanding balance, the remaining amount becomes an unsecured claim against the estate, but if there's no probate estate, that debt will likely go uncollected.

You may choose to return the vehicle voluntarily, especially if it no longer fits your budget or lifestyle. If you're not personally liable for the debt, then the creditor has limited options. But this is not always a simple decision, of course. If the car is your only mode of transportation, for instance, you may think carefully about your options, even when you are not legally obligated to take on the loan. The car may also carry emotional significance that transcends finances. However, what matters most is not what the car meant yesterday but what it costs and contributes today. Of course, if the title was in both of your names, you cannot return the vehicle and expect the loan will be forgiven.

The same principles apply to other types of secured debt, such as RVs, boats, or equipment loans. If the debt is tied to an asset, the lender can repossess it. But your responsibility ends where your legal obligation does. Just because you inherit the asset doesn't mean you automatically inherit the loan. If you want to keep it, of course the debt must be addressed, but if you don't, it's often better to return it and move forward with a clean slate. What makes secured debt different than unsecured debt, such as credit cards or personal loans, is that the lender has recourse. It may not necessarily be against you personally, but against the asset itself. If payments stop, the asset held as collateral can be taken back. So if you want to keep the asset, someone has to pay for it.

In some cases, the value of the car, RV, or boat may be less than the remaining loan balance. When that happens—when the asset is "upside down"—you're faced with more than a legal question. It becomes a financial decision. Does it make sense to continue paying on something that's worth less than what's owed? If you return the vehicle or it's repossessed, the lender will sell it and apply the proceeds to the loan. If there's a remaining balance and no probate estate or you weren't a co-signer, that shortfall is typically written off. In these situations, even if the lender offers you the chance to assume the loan, it's worth pausing to consider whether keeping the asset serves your best financial interest. Just because you can take on the debt doesn't mean you should. You might have the option to take over the loan, especially if the lender is accommodating, but don't do so blindly. Ask yourself, is the asset still useful to you? Can you reasonably afford the payments? Does the loan align with your new financial goals?

Keeping an underwater vehicle for sentimental reasons or out of a sense of obligation is rarely in your best interest. In many cases walking away may be the more rational and freeing choice.

The key takeaway here is that with secured debt you can't inherit an asset without also addressing the loan attached to it. However, that doesn't mean you're automatically responsible for the debt. If you want to keep the car, though, naturally the loan has to be paid. If not, returning the asset may be the cleanest path forward.

MORTGAGES: WHAT HAPPENS TO THE HOUSE AND THE LOAN?

For many households, the mortgage is the largest debt and the most emotionally charged. But just like other liabilities, what happens to it after your spouse's death depends on how the loan and title were structured.

If you and your spouse were both on the mortgage and both on the title, the loan doesn't go away when one spouse dies. As the surviving borrower, you simply continue making payments under the existing terms. You do not need to refinance or requalify, and you have the legal right to remain in the home.

If the mortgage was in your spouse's name only but the home was jointly titled or held in a trust naming you as successor, things may still proceed smoothly. Federal law, specifically the Garn-St. Germain Act, protects surviving spouses and certain heirs from being forced to refinance or pay off the mortgage upon a borrower's death. As long as you inherit the property and plan to occupy it, the lender generally cannot call the loan due simply because of the death.

That said, the protection only extends so far. If the loan wasn't being paid, or you don't have the ability or desire to maintain the home, the lender can still initiate foreclosure. Being protected from immediate payoff doesn't erase the obligation to make monthly payments. If you wish to keep the home but can't afford the current loan, you may need to request a loan assumption or explore a refinance, depending on the lender's policies and your financial situation.

It's also important to distinguish between the mortgage loan and the ownership of the property. If the home was titled solely in your spouse's name and no trust or survivorship mechanism was in place, you may need to go through probate to legally transfer ownership, even if you were married. This can delay your ability to sell, refinance, or manage the property, even if you're willing and able to keep up with the mortgage payments. It also opens a door for unsecured creditors. While credit card debt typically dies with the decedent when there are no estate assets to pursue, probate changes that. If the home becomes part of the probate estate and there aren't sufficient liquid assets to satisfy outstanding debts, unsecured creditors may petition the court to force the sale of the property. This isn't about personal liability. It's about the estate's obligation, and if the home is part of that estate, it can be exposed.

In community property states like California, homes acquired during the marriage are typically considered community property, even if the title was in one spouse's name. However, legal title and loan documents still govern practical access, so if you are not listed on the deed or trust it's critical to take action to secure legal ownership.

If you decide not to keep the home, you do have options. You can sell the property and use the proceeds to pay off the mortgage, or in some cases, negotiate a deed-in-lieu of foreclosure to transfer the home back to the lender. It's essential to understand how title, equity, and debt interact and to know that you must have legal ownership (title) in order to take any action.

Unfortunately, if the title remains unresolved, such as if you remain in the home and neglect to retitle the property or if the estate remains unresolved and still open, the financial and legal issues won't go away.

If you decide to turn your home into a rental property after your spouse's death, it can complicate matters, depending on the type of mortgage. Many loans, especially those with favorable terms like FHA, VA, or first-time homebuyer programs, require you to occupy the home for a certain period, typically one year. Consequently, it could violate the loan agreement if you convert the property to a rental too soon. While lenders don't always enforce these provisions, it's a risk worth understanding. Even for conventional loans, the lender may want to be notified of the change in use. So, before renting it out, review your mortgage documents carefully and contact the lender if you're unsure about any restrictions. Also be aware that converting your home to a rental can have long-term tax consequences, especially if you decide to sell the property later. The rules around exclusions, depreciation, and capital gains can change significantly once the property is no longer your primary residence. It's a good idea to speak with a tax advisor before finalizing your decision so that you fully understand what this choice may mean down the road. Of course you'll also need to update your insurance policy from homeowner's coverage to landlord coverage if you decide to turn it into a rental property.

If your home has a home equity line of credit (HELOC) or a second mortgage, those debts remain in place even after your spouse passes. As the surviving owner or heir, you're responsible for continuing the payments. Most HELOCs function as interest-only loans during the initial draw period, followed by a repayment phase in which both principal and interest must be paid. If you are approaching the repayment phase, your monthly cost could rise significantly. So be sure to factor any adjustments or balloon payments into your cash flow needs as you revise your financial plan.

Because a HELOC is a revolving line of credit, some lenders have clauses that allow them to freeze or reduce the available credit after a death, especially if the loan was based on the deceased spouse's income or credit profile. If your name is not on the HELOC, the lender may even block further draws until the account is formally assumed, refinanced, or paid off. That could be a problem if you were relying on that credit line for home repairs or renovation. Naturally, you'll need to stay current on all payments including your first mortgage, second mortgage, and HELOC, to avoid risk of default or foreclosure since second mortgages and HELOCs, just like primary mortgages, are still tied to the property. Lenders continue to hold a legal claim against it.

Ultimately your decision should balance legal standing, emotional ties, and financial sustainability. The mortgage doesn't disappear, but neither does your right to determine whether keeping the home is the right choice for your future.

WHAT TO DO WITH YOUR SPOUSE'S 401(K)S AND IRAS?

When your spouse passes, you'll need to decide what to do with their retirement accounts. Assuming you are the named beneficiary, if they had an IRA, 401(k) or other qualified plan, the decisions you make can affect your taxes, your income flexibility, and your overall retirement plan. As the surviving spouse, you have options no one else gets. With an IRA, for instance, you can treat it as your own (what's called a spousal IRA) or you can treat it as an inherited (or beneficiary) IRA. Both options come with different rules, and the best choice often comes down to your age and your cash flow needs.

If you're over age 59½, treating the account as your own may be a straightforward option depending on your situation. You can roll his or her IRA, 401(k) or qualified account into your existing IRA, or you can open a new IRA in your name and from there take withdrawals as needed without penalty. You can also delay required minimum distributions (RMDs) until you reach age 73 and manage the money as if it were always yours. But if you're under 59½, and especially if you need to access the funds, treating it as a beneficiary IRA might provide more flexibility. Why? Because you can withdraw from an inherited IRA at any age without the 10 percent early withdrawal penalty. That gives you more flexibility during a potentially tough transition period, especially if you're not working or need to replace your spouse's income. You can later convert a beneficiary IRA into a spousal IRA, but you can't go the other way. That means if you choose to move the account to your own name, you are subject to the age 59½ penalties for early distributions. That's why it's so important to pause and look at your bigger plan before making any decisions. You may decide to treat it as an inherited IRA for now, and roll it into your own IRA later, after you turn 59½.

Now let's talk about 401(k)s. If your spouse had one or more 401(k)s, you might be tempted to just leave them there. But that may not be the most efficient long-term strategy depending on the fees, flexibility, or plan rules. Employer-sponsored plans often have limited investment choices, many layers of fees (sometimes hidden), and fewer withdrawal options. Some even require lump-sum distributions. These plans are generally built for accumulation, not necessarily distribution, and they typically are not built for beneficiaries. As a surviving spouse, you have unique options. You can generally leave it in the plan as a beneficiary (or inherited) 401(k), of course. Or you can treat the account as your own by rolling it into a spousal IRA, or you can establish a beneficiary IRA if that better suits your needs. Either approach can help consolidate accounts, simplify your finances, and reduce complexity. When you're grieving and handling finances on your own, the last thing you need is a spreadsheet full of old, scattered accounts.

Fees are another area where 401(k)s can be less transparent or harder to control. These plans typically carry several layers of fees, some visible, some hidden. You may be paying administrative fees, recordkeeping fees, advisory fees, and fund management fees, all baked into the plan structure. On top of that, there may be transaction fees when you move money. Most of these costs are built into the plan structure, but costs can add up. With an IRA, you may have more flexibility in how you manage costs and choose services. You decide if and how you want to pay for advice. If you work with a financial advisor, you're paying for direct, personalized advice and service, not generic education. And depending on where your IRA is held and how it's structured, you may be able to eliminate or significantly reduce transaction costs and administrative fees. This structure can be more transparent and, depending on the provider and setup, potentially more cost efficient.

If investing isn't your comfort zone, or if you simply don't want to deal with it, this is the time to ask for help. A fiduciary advisor can help you evaluate how to consolidate accounts, explore tax-efficient strategies, and manage your investments in a way that supports your goals. This isn't about being hands-off. It's about being smart with your time, your energy, and your peace of mind.

Whether it's an IRA or a 401(k), the decision you make should support your whole financial life, not just solve a short-term problem. Take a step back, seek informed, personalized guidance, and choose the path that gives you both flexibility and confidence. This stage of life already brings enough emotional and practical complexity. Your finances should bring clarity, not confusion. So whether it's choosing between a spousal IRA and a beneficiary IRA, or deciding how to consolidate and invest inherited retirement accounts, the goal is the same: build a structure that works for you.

REQUIRED MINIMUM DISTRIBUTIONS

This is where things get even more complicated. If you're retired and drawing from pre-tax accounts like IRAs, remember you'll eventually face required minimum distributions (RMDs for short). Depending upon your year of birth, starting at age 73 or age 75 under current law, you are required to withdraw a certain amount from your traditional retirement accounts each year, and those withdrawals count as taxable income. So even if you don't need the money, you're forced to take it and report it on your taxes. If those RMDs push your income higher, they can move you into a higher tax bracket and possibly trigger IRMAA, the Medicare surcharge. That means RMDs can trigger higher income taxes and Medicare premiums, which is why RMD planning, ideally with your advisor, is so important. Your advisor can forecast future RMDs and show how they may affect your taxes overall, helping you prepare in advance and consider strategies to mitigate their impact before they begin.

TAXES

One of the most immediate and often overlooked changes after losing a spouse is the change in your federal income tax filing status. For most people, this change becomes evident during the first full tax year following the death of their spouse because you are no longer considered married for filing purposes and must now file as a single taxpayer or qualifying widow(er), if eligible.

In the year of your spouse's death the IRS allows you to file Married Filing Jointly one final time, assuming you did not remarry during that calendar year. This provides some continued tax advantages, including access to the wider tax brackets, higher standard deduction, and more favorable thresholds for capital gains and IRMAA. However, starting January 1 of the following year, you are typically reclassified as a Single filer, unless you have a dependent child and qualify for the Qualifying Widow(er) with Dependent Child status, which provides joint filing rates for up to two years.

This change in status often results in what's referred to as the "widow's penalty." This is a term used to describe the higher taxes many surviving spouses pay simply because of the shift to the single filing brackets. The trouble is that the tax thresholds for singles are significantly lower, while your income doesn't necessarily drop in step. To make sense of this, let me explain how our income tax system works.

The US tax system is progressive. That means the more you earn, the higher the rate applied to your income as it moves through different tiers, or "brackets." You don't pay one flat rate on all your income. Instead, you pay one rate on the dollars in the first bracket, a higher rate on the next bracket, and so on. As your income progresses upward, more of those dollars fall into the higher brackets and are taxed at higher percentages.

Below you will see the 2026 tax brackets for different types of filers. Notice the 10 percent bracket applies to income from zero to different levels depending on your filing status. Married individuals filing jointly pay 10 percent on the first $24,800 as compared to only $12,400 for single filers. Although that is half of the joint bracket, income as a widow does not usually fall by half because many of your expenses stay the same. That means you may still have similar retirement pensions, IRA withdrawals or required minimum distributions.

This mismatch is what creates the widow's penalty. Your filing thresholds shrink, but your income does not typically shrink in step. That means more of your dollars can get pushed into the higher brackets, raising your tax bill even though your household income has gone down.

2026 Federal Income Tax Brackets and Rates for Single Filers, Married Couples Filing Jointly, and Heads of Household

Tax Rate	For Single Filers	For Married Individuals Filing Joint Returns	For Heads of Households
10%	$0 to $12,400	$0 to $24,800	$0 to $17,700
12%	$12,401 to $50,400	$24,801 to $100,800	$17,701 to $67,450
22%	$50,401 to $105,700	$100,801 to $211,400	$67,451 to $105,700
24%	$105,701 to $201,775	$211,401 to $403,550	$105,701 to $201,775
32%	$201,776 to $256,225	$403,551 to $512,450	$201,776 to $256,200
35%	$256,226 to $640,600	$512,451 to $768,700	$256,201 to $640,600
37%	$640,601 or more	$768,701 or more	$640,601 or more

Source: Internal Revenue Service, "Revenue Procedure 2025–32"

And it's not just the income tax brackets that change. Standard deductions, phase-outs for itemized deductions, and eligibility for certain tax credits and deductions are all recalibrated. The threshold for when Social Security becomes taxable is also lower for single filers. The net investment income tax, capital gains rates, and IRA deduction rules can also be affected, creating a ripple effect across your tax return.

These changes can also affect your Medicare premiums, referred to as IRMAA, which stands for Income Related Monthly

Adjustment Amount. In short, IRMAA is a surcharge based on your Modified Adjusted Gross Income (MAGI) that can increase the cost of your Medicare Part B and Part D coverage. To determine whether you are subject to IRMAA, Social Security looks back at your tax return from two years prior at your Modified Adjusted Gross Income (MAGI) or your adjusted gross income from your tax return with certain deductions and exclusions added back. That is the number Medicare and the IRS use to determine eligibility for programs and surcharges like IRMAA. As a single filer, you will reach the surcharge thresholds sooner than you would have as part of a married couple, potentially raising your Medicare premiums even if your lifestyle has not changed. For 2026, IRMAA kicks in for married couples filing jointly with MAGI of $218,001 or higher, as compared to single filers at $109,001 and higher.

The good news is that IRMAA is not always set in stone. Social Security allows you to appeal if your current income is significantly lower due to certain life-changing events. The approved life-changing events for an IRMAA appeal are:

- Death of a spouse
- Marriage or divorce
- Work stoppage or reduction
- Loss of income-producing property
- Loss or reduction of pension income
- Employer settlement payment

So, as you can see, the year of your spouse's death can offer a narrow but critical planning window. It is your final opportunity to make strategic tax moves such as Roth conversions, harvesting gains, or making deductible contributions, because it is the last year you can still file a joint tax return. It also sets the stage for a future IRMAA appeal, since the death of a spouse is a qualifying life-changing event. That appeal would be filed two years later, when Medicare looks back at your higher income year to calculate IRMAA. You may be able to complete Roth conversions now, and later appeal the Medicare surcharge on the basis of your spouse's death as a qualifying life-changing event. For those with large retirement accounts or taxable investment assets, it can be advantageous to accelerate certain actions during this time before your filing status changes.

Understanding and responding to these tax shifts isn't just about compliance. It's about positioning yourself wisely for the future. Proper tax planning during this transition can reduce your lifetime tax liability, help preserve your wealth, and provide more control over future income. And while taxes may not be top of mind, ignoring them can lead to costly surprises that compound the financial stress of this new phase of life.

State Income Taxes

Depending on where you live, your state may have its own set of brackets and deductions, which also aren't generally as forgiving to single filers. Some states apply the same rules to everyone regardless of marital status, but others mimic the federal code and create the same imbalance, meaning your state tax liability could rise at the same time your federal taxes and Medicare costs go up. It can add up to a double or triple hit to your cash flow, which can be destructive if you're not prepared for it. It can potentially be worse than the hit from inflation.

USING HOLISTIC PLANNING TO MASTER TAX STRATEGY

That's why now is the time to be proactive. The earlier you begin thinking about how your income will be taxed, how your RMDs will affect you, and how to stay below IRMAA thresholds, the more control you have. These days, tax management isn't just for the wealthy. For those widowed, it's a lifeline to protect your income and your lifestyle. It's about preserving the retirement you've built and honoring the financial legacy you shared. By making intentional decisions now, you may be able to reduce the emotional toll and financial disruption later. With tax planning, you can work toward protecting your lifestyle, minimizing surprises, and gaining peace of mind on your terms.

That's also why it's so important to understand not just where you stand today, but where you're headed. The shift from married to single filing status isn't just a tax inconvenience, it's a signal that your financial life has changed in fundamental ways. Your income might stay the same, or even decrease, but your tax burden could still go up. Add in the impact of required IRA distributions, Medicare premiums, and possible changes in your deductions, and suddenly your retirement cash flow looks a lot different than you expected.

Through comprehensive and holistic financial planning, you can be sure strategies are customized based on your goals, needs, resources, and individual situation. In my view a sound financial plan is important, especially as you enter the retirement phase of your life. Based on my experience, too many people step into retirement without a plan at all. To me, that's like building a house without professionally engineered blueprints. Imagine what a home would look like if builders just started hammering together a bunch of lumber. But that's exactly what people do every day. They make major financial decisions without a master plan, whether it's about buying or selling assets, triggering tax liabilities, or structuring their estate plan. Without measuring the full impact or considering your total financial picture, it's difficult to ensure each decision is consistent with your goals and, more specifically, supports the sustainability of your resources.

Strategies should never be conceived in a vacuum. You need to think ahead and look ahead. Just like driving, you don't navigate the road by staring only at what's right in front of you. You're constantly checking your rearview mirror, scanning your surroundings, and anticipating what's coming. Financial planning works the same way. Every move you make should be evaluated within the broader context of your overall plan. It's not enough to simply know the available strategies. You need to understand how to use them in coordination with and to your advantage.

These days there's no shortage of options, but that abundance can quickly lead to choice overload, meaning being overwhelmed by too many paths forward. That often leads to paralysis, with people making no decision at all. Perhaps worse, this can result in rushed decisions without fully understanding the consequences. However, with a comprehensive plan and of course the right advisory team, you are better able to shift from reacting to proactively choosing financial strategies that work *for* you and not against you.

ROTH CONVERSIONS, WITHDRAWAL SEQUENCING AND TAX-AWARE INCOME PLANNING

One of the most common and often misunderstood strategies is the Roth conversion. This is when you move money from a traditional IRA or 401(k) into a Roth IRA. Yes, if you do this, you must pay taxes on that money in the year you convert it, so in essence you are front-loading your taxes, but that means you convert taxable dollars into a Roth account, which can grow tax-free if IRS rules are followed. Withdrawals later in retirement won't increase your taxable income, subject to the five-year holding rule. Why does this matter? Well, first of all, the future of taxes is uncertain, but if you believe, as many of us do, that taxes will likely go up over your lifetime, it's a way to turn uncertainty into certainty. By paying taxes today, you know exactly what you will pay and as long as you follow the Roth conversion rules as defined by the IRS, you may be able to generate tax-free withdrawals in retirement, provided you meet IRS qualifications. Also, once you hit age 73 or RMD age, with traditional IRAs or 401(k)s, forced withdrawals can inflate your income quickly and may bump you into a higher tax bracket or trigger IRMAA. However, by doing strategic Roth conversions, you can reduce your future taxable income and gain more control over your tax situation (and possibly health care costs) in later years, because Roth distributions are not currently included in IRMAA calculations under current tax law. So it's not about avoiding taxes, but rather choosing when and how you pay them. Having a mix of account types with different tax treatments may provide more flexibility in managing taxes and income sustainability.

Beyond Roth Conversions, another essential consideration is deciding from where you pull your retirement income. Most people with significant savings have money spread across different types of accounts, such as traditional tax-deferred IRAs, Roth IRAs, and taxable brokerage accounts. Each has different tax consequences. Being intentional about which accounts you draw from, and in what order, is one of the most effective ways to reduce your tax bill in retirement.

For example, if you draw from your brokerage account in a year when you're trying to keep your income low (perhaps to avoid IRMAA) you might pay lower capital gains taxes than if you pulled from an IRA. Or you might combine withdrawals from both tax-deferred and Roth accounts to smooth out your income and avoid bumping into a higher bracket. These aren't decisions to make on the fly. In fact, they shouldn't be made in isolation at all.

Every move, whether it's rolling over a 401(k), choosing between a spousal or inherited IRA, or consolidating accounts, should be part of a broader income strategy that takes into account taxes, timing, risk tolerance, and your long-term goals.

And this is where working with a professional is not just helpful, it may be smart. We've worked with thousands of individuals transitioning into and through retirement, and I've seen the same mistakes made time and time again. People rushing decisions, overlooking tax traps, missing opportunities to simplify, or failing to match their investments with their new reality. You don't get a redo, so take the time to plan well. Surround yourself with the right people. And make decisions that aren't just about what's easiest right now, but what's best for your future.

If you're age 70½ or older and you're charitably inclined, a Qualified Charitable Distribution, or QCD, can be a smart tool to consider. A QCD allows you to give directly to a qualified charity from your IRA, and that distribution is not included in your taxable income. That means it can help satisfy your RMD without raising your income, which can help you avoid higher tax brackets or IRMAA surcharges. It's also a way to support causes you care about while also making a strategic tax decision.

And then there's loss harvesting. If you have a taxable investment account and some of your holdings have dropped in value, you might be able to sell those positions to realize the loss. That loss can then be used to offset gains you have realized or eventually will likely have to realize elsewhere. Meanwhile, you can reduce your ordinary income by up to $3,000 in a given year, or better yet, this strategy can enable you to enjoy tax-free retirement income.

I'll never forget when Rich called me one day and said, "I guess I have to accept that now that I'm 65, I just won't have to pay taxes anymore." I paused for a moment, confused, until

I realized what he meant. He had completely misunderstood the tax strategy we had put in place years earlier. Back during the Great Recession of 2008, we harvested losses in his portfolio and banked them for future use. So when the market eventually recovered and we sold securities at a gain, his tax professional was able to offset those gains with the losses we had captured years earlier. The result? Rich had tax-free retirement income for three years. I had warned him when we set up this strategy that it wouldn't last forever. I explained it was a temporary benefit from a tough market environment, but after a few years of no tax liability he got used to it and assumed that tax-free income would continue indefinitely.

It's a good reminder that tax strategies aren't permanent. They're opportunities, often time-limited, but they need to be part of a long-term plan. If you're not working with someone who understands how to capture and use those opportunities when they come around, you may miss them or forget how they work entirely.

Keep in mind that tax-loss harvesting can be especially useful in volatile or down markets, when sharp swings create opportunities to sell investments at a loss and capture that loss for tax purposes. Those losses can later be used to offset gains when you sell appreciated investments, allowing you to rebalance a concentrated position with less tax impact or free up funds for income without creating an immediate tax bill.

Suppose, for example, the market experiences a 20 percent correction and your taxable (non-IRA) account falls by $200,000. If you sell those positions at a loss relative to their purchase price, you can capture and carry those losses forward for future use. Now imagine a few years later you own stocks that have grown by more than $100,000 each, but you hesitate to sell because of the tax bill. With tax losses carried forward, you can offset those gains, allowing you to sell, rebalance to reduce portfolio risk, or free up funds to support your retirement income, you would only owe tax on gains that exceed the $200,000 in tax losses you banked earlier.

Just be careful with the "wash sale" rule which says if you sell an investment at a loss and then buy the same or a substantially identical security within 30 days before or after the sale, the IRS will disallow the loss for tax purposes. And keep in mind that tax-loss harvesting only applies to taxable investment accounts. Retirement accounts such as IRAs and 401(k)s are tax-deferred, so gains and losses inside those accounts are not reportable for tax purposes.

Now I want to pause here and add something important. What I've just described are foundational tools that can benefit many widows in retirement. But if your situation is more complex, for example if you are dealing with substantial capital gains, multiple real estate holdings, legacy planning goals, or a business interest, then you will need to go further. There are additional, more advanced tax strategies that may apply to your situation such as donor-advised funds, charitable trusts, structured installment sales, and other income-deferral or income-smoothing techniques that go well beyond the basics.

This is exactly why I believe no one should make these decisions alone. Your situation is unique. Your goals, your income, your assets, and your values create a combination that is uniquely yours. So while it's incredibly important to understand these tax strategies and how they work, it's may be even more important to talk them through with a qualified advisor who can look at the full picture and guide you toward the most appropriate, tax-efficient path. Tax planning is not just a year-by-year decision. It's a long-term strategy. And when done right, it doesn't just protect your retirement, it empowers it.

While one of the biggest financial shocks many widows face is how quickly their tax situation can change, it does not have to be a lasting setback. The widow's penalty, required minimum distributions, Medicare surcharges, and state taxes may be complicated, but with the right planning they are manageable. The more proactive you are, the more control you will have over what you keep, how your income is structured, and how your legacy is carried forward. Knowledge and preparation will not erase the pain of loss, but they will give you the confidence to move forward with clarity and strength.

CHAPTER SEVEN

How to Protect Your Future

From Predators, Poor Advice, and Costly Mistakes

Guarding your future starts with asking the hard questions.

There's something that happens after you lose a spouse. The world doesn't just see you as vulnerable, it often sees you as *available*. Available for advice. Available for influence. Available for persuasion. And unfortunately, in too many cases, available to be taken advantage of.

No one likes to think they're susceptible to manipulation, but grief has a way of softening your guard. When you're emotionally raw, mentally taxed, and struggling to get through each day, your guard is naturally down. And that's exactly when the opportunists show up. Some are strangers with slick pitches. Others are familiar faces like family, friends, or neighbors who might mean well, but still push too hard, assume too much, or ask for too much. In the quiet after loss, you may feel pressure to be agreeable, to trust, or to make decisions quickly just to be done with it all. But this is a time to protect your space, your money, and your future with care.

We've seen too many widows and widowers, thoughtful and capable people, make decisions they later regretted. Not because they were reckless, but because they were overwhelmed, emotionally exhausted, or simply trying to do the right thing. Maybe it was signing off on an investment they didn't understand. Maybe it was lending money to a child or friend they felt too guilty to say no to. Maybe it was trusting the wrong salesperson because the pitch sounded polished and reassuring. The results range from disappointing to devastating, and most of them could have been avoided with one simple rule: slow down and verify everything.

You, and you alone now, are the steward and the gatekeeper of your financial well-being. Not every decision needs to be made right now, and always remember that not every opportunity is what it seems. Not everyone who steps in to help is truly qualified, and some are not even honest. That may sound harsh, but it's a reality I've witnessed far too often. This is not to say you should become fearful or paranoid. Rather, be mindful of the need to pause, ask questions, trust your instincts, and seek second opinions before you move forward with anything that affects your long-term financial health.

Of course, protecting your future isn't just about money. It's about peace of mind. It's about preserving what you and your spouse built together. It's about safeguarding your independence and your ability to make choices from a place of strength, not stress. Whether you've just begun to manage things on your own or you've always been financially involved, this is the time to draw firm, clear boundaries, and to recognize that protecting yourself is not selfish. It's smart. It's necessary. And it's absolutely your right.

The most common traps we see people fall into are often avoidable. Predatory behavior can hide behind charm. Weak or conflicted advice isn't always easy to recognize. Building a protective team around you means you don't have to face big decisions on your own. Financial strength is not just about growth and planning. It is also about defense, protecting yourself, recognizing bad advice, and avoiding costly mistakes. And now, more than ever, you deserve a strategy that delivers on both.

UNDERSTANDING FINANCIAL VULNERABILITY AFTER LOSS

There is a window of time, and it's usually the first 12 to 18 months after a spouse dies, when surviving spouses are at their most vulnerable financially. This isn't because they've suddenly lost intellectual capacity or capability. It's because grief changes your brain. You're overwhelmed, tired, foggy, and emotionally stretched. Your decision-making is slower. Your intuition is dulled. And your defenses are down. Scammers and opportunists recognize this vulnerability, and they look for ways to take advantage. Some of them are strangers, some are acquaintances, and occasionally they might even be family. But what they all are betting is that you're not at your best.

One of the most heartbreaking patterns I've seen is online romance scams. It's more common than many realize. A woman I once knew, let's call her Mary, lost her spouse of 38 years. She went to a dating website out of loneliness. Someone reached out. He was kind, attentive, and said all the right things. He claimed to be a contractor working overseas. He said he was widowed too. After weeks of daily text messages and phone calls, she began to feel emotionally connected to him. He said all the right things, filled her quiet days with laughter and hope. He promised to come visit, and she believed him. But something always came up. A delayed contract, a banking problem, an unexpected legal issue. And slowly she began sending money to "help him out." It started small, but then it grew. By the time she realized what was happening, she had wired more than $60,000. He always had a reason why he could not come see her. And she finally understood she had been scammed. She felt embarrassed, ashamed, and heartbroken, not only because of the money but because the relationship she believed was real was nothing more than a carefully crafted lie. We have seen more than one client fall victim to these kinds of romance scams, I'm afraid.

But it doesn't have to be a stranger to cause damage. I've also seen "friend-of-the-family" business pitches show up right after a loss. Someone who "knew your spouse," maybe even a distant family member, reaches out with a business idea they claim will honor your spouse's memory. They might say it is a way to carry on a legacy and invite you to invest or be involved. There's often flattery involved. And sentimentality. And urgency. Before you know it you're being asked to invest in something that is very risky with no independent verification, and which has no place in your long-term plan. It's easy to get pulled in, especially if they say things like, "Your husband believed in me" or "Auntie wanted to do this."

Then there are the sudden charitable requests. Many are often genuine in appearance, but poorly timed or emotionally manipulative. Sometimes people assume that because you've lost a spouse, you have money to spare or a legacy to give. Sometimes it's an obscure nonprofit. Other times it's a local fundraiser or even a well-meaning friend asking you to contribute to a cause their heart is set on. Giving is beautiful. But giving while you're still navigating grief needs to be intentional, not reactive.

Grief doesn't just open you up to strangers, I'm afraid. It can also complicate relationships with the people closest to you. And while it's difficult to admit, sometimes that includes your own children.

In our experience we've found that most adult children are loving, respectful, and deeply protective of their surviving parent. They show up, they support, and they help in ways that honor the loss and lift the burden. But I'm afraid we have also seen situations that are subtle at first, but where grief creates an opening for pressure, persuasion, or guilt. It's not always malicious. Sometimes it's just a child who is scared, distressed, or who wants to grab onto something like money, control, or promises in order to feel more secure.

It can start small. An adult child who says, "Dad would've wanted me to have that," or "You don't need that big of a house now, maybe you should sell it and help us buy one." Sometimes it's more direct, like asking for early access to an inheritance, requesting to be added to a deed or bank account, or wanting a "loan" that doesn't feel like it can be repaid. And often it's layered with emotion, including grief, love, or even fear, which makes it harder to say no.

What makes this dynamic especially hard is that most people think *my kids would never do that*. And hopefully that's true, but even good kids can make bad decisions when they're grieving, or when they see an opening that benefits them. The pressure may not come with raised voices or demands. It may come through tears, through subtle well-timed comments, or through persistent nudging that wears you down when you are already exhausted.

That's why it's so important to pause before giving away control, money, or access. This isn't about trusting your children or others, but because right now you need space to protect yourself *first*. You need time to make decisions with confidence, not obligation. And sometimes the best way to show your love is to maintain a boundary—not out of mistrust, but out of wisdom.

If you're feeling torn or unsure, bring in a third party. There are plenty available, be it a fiduciary advisor, attorney, or someone else who can help guide the conversation in a neutral way. Protecting your future isn't selfish. It's how you ensure that you can continue to support your family and yourself on your terms and with intention, confidence, and peace of mind.

Some may dismiss this and wonder if it really happens. How do smart, capable people fall into these traps? The truth is, it happens often. And even if you believe you would never fall victim, it's still important to be knowledgeable, because awareness is one of the best protections you have.

You see, grief often plays tricks on our internal compass. It amplifies our desire to connect, to feel useful, to experience something warm at a time when emptiness may prevail. You might say yes to something because you want to *feel* again, to feel needed, to feel understood, to feel loved, or even to feel included. That is what predators prey on, the emotional gaps that are so common during grief.

For many, this is also the first time they are financially independent. It's the first time in decades that they have not had anyone to run things by or get a second opinion at the dinner table. So when someone comes along and says, "I've got you," or "I'm here to help," it can feel like a relief. However, that's when the walls start to come down, and when you stop listening to your instincts and start listening to their voice. And for friends or family members who have greedy desires, whether they admit it or not, well, they seem to know that you're more likely to say yes right now. They sense the hesitation, the loneliness, the need for connection. They know you might be too exhausted to argue, or too overwhelmed to weigh the long-term consequences. So they push. Not always with force, but with timing, guilt, or familiarity. And because they're close to you, it's even harder to separate your emotions from the decision at hand.

This is when you need to be especially careful. It's easy to confuse familiarity with trust. Just because someone's been in your life for years doesn't mean they're the right person to guide you through a financial choice. That includes adult children, siblings, in-laws, and lifelong friends. It's not about assuming bad intentions. It's about recognizing that grief reshuffles the emotional deck and sometimes people see opportunity where they should see the need for restraint.

This doesn't mean you close yourself off or push people away. It means you protect the space between their request and your response. You slow down. You say, "Let me think about that" or "I'd like to run this by someone first." Give yourself room to hear your own voice before acting on someone else's. This shows your strength and control despite your grief. That alone may defuse the pressure or prevent a misstep entirely. However, it's also why you need structure, boundaries, and support. You need a pause button, like a rule that says, "I don't make major financial decisions alone right now," or "Everything gets reviewed by my advisor first." Again, it's not paranoia. It's about protection. It's about prudence. Whether your trusted advisor is your attorney, accountant, financial advisor, or even your pastor, having that sounding board protects you from making decisions in the heat of the moment. And it could be the difference between preserving what you've built and watching it slowly unravel at the hands of someone who may never have had your best interest at heart.

SPOTTING PREDATORY BEHAVIOR DISGUISED AS HELP

The most dangerous predators rarely look like villains. They often show up with a smile, a warm tone, and just the right words to make you feel cared for. They don't storm through the front door. In fact, they offer to carry your groceries, fix something in the yard, or "help you sort things out." They know how to seem like exactly what you need, a companion, a comfort, a steady hand. But what they're really after is access. To your trust. To your vulnerability. And to your money.

It could be someone new, like a person you meet at a grief group or online who quickly becomes attentive and overly involved. Or it could be someone familiar who steps in and starts offering help you didn't ask for. I've seen these people call themselves "financial advocates," "spiritual companions," or even "friends of your late spouse." Sometimes they are your own "friends." They offer to review your paperwork, connect you to "their guy," or manage your affairs "just until you get back on your feet." But there's a difference between real support and a disguised agenda. The red flags often show up in the language:

- Your husband would've wanted you to do this.
- Let me take care of that for you, it's too much for you right now.
- You don't need to tell anyone—it's your money.
- You've been through so much. Let me handle this.

That last one is especially dangerous, because it plays into your exhaustion and grief. And yes, it can feel like a relief to let someone else take the wheel for a bit, but at what cost?

Emotional manipulation doesn't always look aggressive. Often, it's subtle. It could take years to develop but it preys on your desire to feel secure, needed, or even loved. I've seen women lured into toxic relationships by men who claimed they were looking for "something real" after their own loss. And I've seen men targeted by "friendly helpers" who slowly became fixtures in their lives, and eventually on their account titles.

It gets even harder when the person trying to "help" is someone you know. A niece offering to move in and help manage the house who later starts using your credit card. A son who insists he should handle your finances but resents every boundary you set. A friend who keeps mentioning a "great investment opportunity" and gets your money but never gives you anything in writing.

At some point generosity becomes expectation, and expectation becomes exploitation. If someone seems offended when you ask questions, seek outside opinions, or take your time, that's a sign that their interest may not be aligned with your wellbeing. True helpers are patient. They are transparent. They respect your timeline and your autonomy.

This is where healthy boundaries come in. You don't owe anyone immediate trust, access, or explanation. You're allowed to say, *I appreciate the offer, but I need to review this with my advisor,* or *I'm not making any financial decisions right now.* And if someone keeps pushing after that, it's a cue to distance yourself. In this state of vulnerability, your peace is worth protecting. So is your financial future. And if someone is offended by your boundaries, they were likely counting on you not having any.

Ellen, my client for nearly a decade, lost her husband after a long marriage. They had built a life together, and in the wake of his passing she found herself deeply lonely. Not long after, a distant family member entered the picture. This was someone I had never heard of in all the years I'd worked with Ellen. However, she suddenly became very present, very involved, and very persuasive. One day, completely out of the blue, I received notice that Ellen had walked into another firm and submitted paperwork to transfer her accounts. I was stunned. There had been no warning, no conversation, no dissatisfaction on her part. We had worked closely and built a trusting relationship for decades, before and through the loss of her husband. I called her, concerned and confused, and as we spoke I could hear someone in the background. It was the newly reunited family member prompting her.

I managed to arrange a meeting with Ellen and, no surprise, the "caring" family member came along. That day Ellen told me she wanted to buy a house for her. A home down the street had come on the market, and now there was this urgent, emotional pull to purchase it so this caring relative could live nearby. It seemed to give Ellen a sense of renewed purpose, a way to feel connected and cared for again. But the more we discussed it, red flags kept waving.

I asked her carefully: "How will you afford the upkeep like property taxes, insurance, repairs?" I gently reminded Ellen that if she bought this house, she wouldn't just be giving a one-time gift. She could be signing up for a long-term financial commitment because this individual had limited income and no clear plan for self-sufficiency. It was evident the expectation wasn't just that Ellen would buy the house, but that she would continue supporting her. But Ellen didn't see it that way.

I encouraged Ellen to consider another approach. "If you want to help," I said, "maybe offer some financial support toward a down payment, but let her carry the rest. Give her the gift of responsibility. Let her build strength, not dependency." I meant every word. The best gifts are often the ones that empower, not enable. But Ellen, motivated by loneliness and the promise of companionship, bought the house for her outright. She imagined holiday dinners, a renewed closeness, and a sense of family just a few doors away.

Tragically, not long after moving in, this individual passed away unexpectedly and in her will she left the house not to Ellen, but to her boyfriend. Now that house down the street belongs to a man Ellen barely knows and who has a revolving cast of girlfriends. They don't wave. They don't say hello. They don't acknowledge her presence. And every day, Ellen has to look at a house she paid for, meant as a gesture of love, companionship and legacy, now occupied by strangers who have no connection to her or the life she imagined.

RED FLAGS IN FINANCIAL ADVICE AND SALES PITCHES

Not all threats to your financial security come from obvious scammers. Some come dressed in suits, with business cards, polished websites, and smooth language. They call themselves advisors, strategists, planners, or consultants. And while some of them are legitimate, others are operating with one goal in mind. They want to sell you something you don't understand, don't need, or can't afford.

One of the biggest warning signs is urgency. If someone says, "You need to act now," or "This is a limited-time opportunity," stop right there. Good financial decisions don't require panic. Be cautious of anyone pressuring you into an investment, insurance policy, or annuity using phrases like "guaranteed returns," "no risk," or "you'll miss out." High-pressure tactics and overly optimistic language are red flags that warrant a second opinion, especially when the product being offered directly benefits the person selling it.

I've seen retirees end up in annuities they didn't fully understand, speculative investments with limited liquidity, products with high surrender charges or steep transaction costs, or complex investments that weren't aligned with their goals, all because the opportunity was framed as safe, exclusive, or time-sensitive.

Another major red flag is discouraging second opinions. If someone tells you not to run their recommendation past your advisor, attorney, or CPA, that's your cue to walk away. You deserve time and space to understand what you're being offered, and that includes reviewing it with people you trust. Anyone who resists transparency most likely isn't looking out for your best interest. In fact, they may be counting on you being isolated, overwhelmed, or too polite to push back. A trustworthy professional will never be offended by your questions. They'll welcome a second set of eyes. They'll provide written materials, clear breakdowns of costs and fees, and full transparency about their role. Most importantly, they'll respect your pace.

So How Do You Know Who's Truly Qualified?

Start by understanding their credentials and compensation model. Titles like "financial advisor" can mean different things. For instance, some financial professionals are fiduciary advisors, while others may be brokers or representatives of financial institutions. The distinction is important.

The fiduciary standard is the highest legal standard in the financial industry. It requires an advisor to put your interests ahead of their own *in every recommendation*. A broker or non-fiduciary advisor may follow what is called the "Best Interest rule," which sounds similar but is not the same. Under this rule, their advice should be in your best interest at the time, but they can still consider their own compensation or their firm's priorities. In other words, it is not the same as being legally bound to act solely for you.

Another way to consider this is that when an advisor is acting in a fiduciary capacity, they are compensated only through fees paid by the client. They do not receive commissions from product sales. If an advisor earns a commission on a transaction, they are not acting in a fiduciary capacity for that transaction. Therefore, when interviewing a prospective advisor, consider asking:

- Are you a fiduciary at all times when working with me?
- How are you compensated—do you receive fees from me, commissions from product providers, or both?
- Can I see a breakdown of all fees and expenses in writing?
- Do you work with a third-party custodian (like Schwab or Fidelity) where I can independently view and track my accounts?

You should also look for certifications that reflect advanced training and a commitment to the highest professional standards. The CERTIFIED FINANCIAL PLANNER™ (CFP®) designation is widely recognized as the gold standard in personal financial planning. To earn it, an advisor must complete a rigorous course of study, pass a comprehensive exam, meet significant professional experience requirements, and commit to ongoing continuing education. CFP® professionals also pledge to follow a strict code of ethics. But, still, no credential can guarantee integrity or alignment with your values, so always combine credentials with your own judgment and a healthy dose of due diligence.

If something feels off, or you find yourself feeling rushed, confused, or uncertain, take that as your cue to pause. Ask for everything in writing. Sleep on it. Talk it through with someone you trust. And remind yourself that you are under no obligation to agree to anything on the spot, no matter how helpful or persuasive someone may seem.

It's not just investment professionals or brokers you have to be cautious about. Financial pressure can also come from other types of professionals, including real estate agents, car salespeople, even funeral coordinators. These individuals may present themselves with warmth, urgency, and helpful language, but when you're grieving emotional vulnerability can make even well-meant suggestions feel overwhelming or lead to decisions that don't serve your long-term best interest.

Real estate agents may suggest now is the time to sell your home, especially if it's "too big for one person" or "filled with difficult memories." They might show you smaller properties, suggest investment properties, or claim there's a buyer already lined up with a cash offer. And while selling your home might eventually be the right decision, doing so too soon can create regrets you can't undo. If you're still grieving, still adjusting, still unsure, your best move may be to wait. Real estate agents are not typically compensated for helping you navigate the emotional complexity behind any buy or sell decisions.

My client, Tom, was in the early stages of dementia. He still drove. He still managed his day-to-day life. But behind the scenes his memory was slipping, his judgment was wavering, and his ability to weigh decisions had quietly begun to erode. But he was living independently.

One afternoon Tom visited a new model home development just a few blocks from where he lived. His current home had recently been remodeled and he was very happy with it as I understood it, but during that visit to these model homes he was convinced, perhaps by a skilled salesperson or perhaps by the polished, persuasive atmosphere, that he needed to start fresh. Somehow, it was concluded this brand-new house was his next step. Commissions were earned on both sides of the transaction, selling his home and buying this new one, yet it appeared that little thought had been given to whether this move truly served Tom's long-term interests. Had proper due diligence been completed, taking into account his emotional state and financial goals, it's likely the decision to sell might have been reconsidered.

Worse, neither his family nor I, his long-time financial advisor, had any idea he had moved. Tom had suddenly gone quiet.

He stopped answering calls and texts. Whether it was confusion, paranoia, or something else entirely, we didn't know. What we learned was that for nearly six months, Tom lived in that new house surrounded by unpacked boxes. The refrigerator was nearly empty. The rooms were bare. He was disoriented, isolated, and clearly confused, barely understanding where he was or how he had gotten there.

This is the quiet side of financial vulnerability that often goes unseen. It's not always dramatic or criminal. Sometimes it's the simple, tragic reality of someone in cognitive decline being influenced, or even just nudged, into a decision they would never have made if their full faculties had been intact. And the legal protections around these decisions are often murky. Unless someone has been declared legally incompetent, they can still sell, buy, sign, and agree.

Tom's story is a cautionary one. If you find yourself feeling unusually withdrawn, making big decisions quickly, or tuning out the people who've always had your back, pause. These may be signs of emotional overload or something more serious, like cognitive decline creeping in. Vulnerability doesn't always look dramatic. Sometimes it's quiet and internal, and disguised as independence. That's why it matters to build in safeguards, like including people you trust when it comes to daily communications, creating systems that slow you down, and structures that help protect you if your thinking becomes cloudy. The earlier you recognize the signs, the better.

Car salespeople are another group to be mindful of. If you've inherited your spouse's car or if they were the one who always handled those decisions, you may feel unsure about what to do next. A good salesperson will guide you gently. But a pushy one may try to steer you into a car you don't need, can't afford, or aren't ready to commit to. You might hear things like, *This deal won't last*, or *I had another buyer interested, but I'll hold it for you.*

Remember, if you're not 100 percent sure why you're making a purchase, it's okay to do nothing. Let your emotions settle before making financial commitments.

Even funeral homes or pre-need sales reps who often work with the bereaved can upsell services, packages, or expensive arrangements under the guise of honoring your loved one. While many are compassionate and respectful, some may still encourage more than you truly want or need. If you ever feel guilty, rushed, or emotionally pressured into overspending, stop. Ask for all costs in writing. Seek a second opinion if necessary. You have the right to slow down, even in moments that feel urgent.

And don't forget insurance agents or bank employees who may offer to "review your accounts" or "make sure you're taken care of." Sometimes these reviews are simply part of good service. Other times they are looking for opportunities to sell products you weren't seeking out. In some cases the offer is well intended, but in others it may be driven by sales goals or incentives. Either way, make sure your decisions are based on careful consideration, not just the comfort of someone's attention or reassurance in a vulnerable moment.

In all of these situations, the test is simple: Are you being given space, or are you being pushed? Are your questions being answered, or redirected? Are you being asked to sign something quickly or invited to take your time? It's not about distrusting everyone. It's about staying alert. Professionals may be polished and practiced, but no one has the right to pressure you into decisions that don't feel fully understood, well considered, or right for your situation.

How to Say No—and Mean It

One of the most powerful tools you can develop at this point in your life isn't a financial product or a legal document. It's a two-letter word: NO. And yet, it can be one of the hardest to say. Especially when you're grieving, tired, and emotionally exposed. Saying no doesn't always feel strong. It can feel awkward, selfish, even disloyal. But the truth is, saying no isn't rejection, it's protection. It's how you hold the line between what serves you and what drains you.

You might be asked to make a loan to someone you love. To co-sign on a debt. To invest in a cousin's business idea. To gift a down payment. To donate to a cause that matters to someone else. And these requests often come from people who mean well, or at least say they do. But just because someone is close to you doesn't mean their request is in *your* best interest. That's why it's essential to separate the person from the ask.

Saying no doesn't mean slamming the door. It can be graceful. It can be kind. It can even be loving. For some people saying no comes easily, but I have found that many people, especially during stressful times, find it difficult to say no. But no can be: *I need time to think this through. I don't make financial decisions quickly anymore.* Or *I've worked hard to protect my future. I'm not in a position to take on any new commitments.* Or *I'd like to help emotionally, but financially, this isn't something I can do.* Or *I have a life insurance policy already. I don't make changes without reviewing it with my advisor first.*

My go-to phrase with aggressive salespeople is, "I'm all set, thank you." With family, it's usually, "If you need a good ear, you know I'm here for you." These phrases are tools, meant to empower you, not to make excuses. They buy you time, set expectations, and remind others (and yourself) that you're allowed to have boundaries, even with people you care deeply about.

What about when a conversation or pitch just feels off? Maybe someone's being too vague. Maybe you feel rushed. Maybe they're name-dropping, promising returns, or brushing off your questions. You don't have to argue. You don't have to explain. You can simply smile and say: *Thank you for the information, but I don't make decisions in meetings like this.* You can say, *I'm going to take this home and review it on my own time.* Or *I've learned that if something can't wait, it's probably not right for me.* Or *I appreciate the time. I'll be in touch if I decide to move forward,* and then walk away. You don't owe anyone more than that.

Perhaps the hardest no of all is with adult children or family members, especially when they are your emotional anchor. But you must remember that you are not their financial plan, and you are not selfish for putting your own needs first. In fact it's often the most loving thing you can do because it creates clarity and stability for everyone involved. You can still be supportive. You can still be generous. But only if it doesn't compromise your own financial security and peace of mind.

I recently met a man who is far behind in his retirement savings due to various challenges he and his wife have faced over the years. His wife is unable to work due to health issues, and he's also supporting a fully capable 26-year-old son who does not work. As a result, his financial obligations are far greater than he can afford. He asked whether filing early for Social Security might help ease the burden, since he's currently covering all household expenses on his own. I explained that while filing early may offer short-term relief, it comes with long-term costs, both to his own retirement income and to the survivor benefits his wife would eventually rely on. What he hadn't fully acknowledged was that the most sustainable solution might be for his adult son to get to work and support himself. This was a clear example of a father who has not yet learned to say no and who, by avoiding that boundary, may be putting both his and his wife's financial future at risk.

You've already been through enough. You don't need to feel guilty for exercising discernment. Saying no doesn't mean you don't care. But it does mean you care enough about yourself to make thoughtful choices, and enough about your relationships to protect them from future resentment or strain. So go ahead. Say no—firmly, kindly, and without apology. You've earned the right to choose what's best for you.

Thoughtful Ways to Say No

No one really likes to say no. It's uncomfortable. Assertive. Awkward, even. Especially when you're already emotionally raw or trying to keep the peace. And this is often how people find themselves in difficult situations. But saying no isn't selfish, it's necessary. It's a skill that protects your time, your energy, and your future. And like any skill, it gets easier with practice. If you have trouble saying no, pick one firm way to say no and use it again and again. It won't sound repetitive. It will sound firm. Here is a list of different ways to say no firmly, kindly, and without apology:

- "I'm not in a place to make that kind of decision right now."
- "I've given it thought, and I need to pass."
- "That's not something I can take on at this stage in my life."
- "No, thank you—I'm focusing on my own stability right now."
- "I appreciate you thinking of me, but I'm going to decline."
- "I'm setting some new boundaries, and this doesn't align with them."
- "This isn't right for me, even if it seems like a good opportunity."
- "I've already committed to what feels right for my future."

- "I need to prioritize what's best for my long-term well-being."
- "Out of respect for myself and my goals, I'm going to have to say no."

THE DANGER OF DIY WHEN YOU'RE EMOTIONALLY DEPLETED

After loss it's completely natural to crave control. Something vital has been taken from you, something that gave your life structure and certainty. So you start *doing:* paying bills, sorting papers, telling yourself *I've got this*. But grief and exhaustion can quietly cloud your thinking, even when you feel capable. That's when doing everything yourself, especially complex financial, legal, or tax decisions, can backfire. Emotional depletion narrows your perspective, making quick decisions feel like progress when they may not be. What seems like clarity in the moment might later reveal itself as confusion in disguise. And that's how unintended consequences arise, often unnoticed until months or even years have passed.

Take taxes, for example. I once knew a woman who, shortly after her husband died, decided to sell the vacation home they had purchased 30 years earlier. She thought she was simplifying her life. But what she didn't realize was that the step-up in basis she had received as a widow only applied to half the property because of how the title was held. By selling quickly and without consulting a tax advisor, she triggered six figures in capital gains taxes. If she had discussed her options she might have been able to pursue alternative strategies or restructured the ownership before selling, and ultimately her tax burden could have been dramatically less.

Another client added her adult daughter to the title of her house because she thought it would "make things easier" if something happened to her. What she didn't realize was that doing so gave her daughter legal rights to the property immediately and compromised her own protection. Years later, when her daughter went through a divorce, the home the client still lived in became a point of contention in the legal proceedings. She had unintentionally placed her own security at risk. She did it out of love, but without the right advice.

Even something as seemingly simple as distributing inherited IRAs can become a problem if not handled properly. Choosing the wrong withdrawal method or mislabeling a transfer can lead to unexpected taxes, penalties, and lost income. In today's multifaceted tax environment, retirement accounts are subject to layers of complicated rules, and a wrong move can't always be undone.

The takeaway is that you don't have to prove anything by doing it all yourself. Even if you've always been the "numbers person" in the relationship. Even if you feel confident. Especially if you feel tired or overwhelmed. Having a second set of eyes, be it a financial advisor, CPA, or estate attorney, doesn't mean giving up control. It means ensuring that your intentions are honored and your assets are preserved, not compromised by limited bandwidth. No one expects you to be an expert in every area of your life. That's why professionals exist. And with this stress, leaning on that support is just smart.

YOUR FINANCIAL GATEKEEPERS: WHO THEY ARE, AND WHY YOU NEED THEM

When you're managing your finances alone for the first time, every decision rests on your shoulders, which can feel like a heavy weight. And while the sense of independence might feel empowering at times, it can also be isolating. The truth is, you're not meant to do all of this alone. Even the most capable people need experts around them. CEOs have boards of directors and financial officers; professional athletes have coaches, trainers, and agents; surgeons consult with teams during complex procedures. Especially when emotions are high, the rules are complicated, and decisions carry lasting consequences, having the right experts by your side isn't a luxury, it's a necessity.

That's where your financial gatekeepers come in. These aren't just people you call when something goes wrong. These are the professionals who help you prevent problems before they happen. They act as buffers between you and the chaos of grief-driven decisions, opportunistic pitches, and avoidable missteps. And, no, you need not be rich and famous in order to assemble your team.

Financial Advisor

Why do you need a financial advisor? Because managing your financial life is about more than crunching numbers. It's about making choices, sometimes emotional, sometimes complex, that impact your future security and peace of mind. An advisor is there to provide expertise, guidance, and clarity, which I believe is always important but can be particularly critical when you have substantial savings and you're overwhelmed. They can help you maintain perspective when you're too close to the problem, and their expertise can help you avoid costly mistakes. They help you see the big picture, think several steps ahead, and stay focused on what truly matters—not just today, but five, ten, twenty years down the road.

It goes without saying that your advisor should be someone you trust. You need someone who helps you manage your wealth in alignment with your values and also communicates clearly. You want an advisor who explains strategies in understandable terms, is transparent about their fees, and keeps you informed throughout the process. Ideally you will work with a fiduciary, someone who is legally required to act in your best interest, rather than a professional who earns commissions and is only required to meet the suitability standard that applies to brokers in certain contexts. It's important to understand what standard your advisor is operating under, because it can directly affect the recommendations you receive and the long-term outcomes you experience.

Fiduciary advisors are required to be clear about their fees and transparent in how they arrive at their recommendations. They work on a fee-only basis, which means they're compensated for their advice rather than for product sales. This structure can reduce potential conflicts of interest and often supports a more patient, planning-based relationship. That said, some professionals, known as hybrid advisors, may operate under both fiduciary and broker-dealer roles. This dual registration can create confusion for clients, especially if it's unclear which standard is being applied at any given moment. For this reason, it's wise to ask questions and ensure you fully understand how your advisor is compensated and what obligations they have to you under the law.

Unfortunately, fiduciary advice is still not the norm across the financial services industry. It requires a high level of commitment, expertise, and client-focused thinking that not all professionals provide. Further, some firms do not permit their advisors to act as fiduciaries. A qualified fee-only fiduciary advisor can help you manage investments, plan for retirement, address tax considerations, design income strategies, and offer perspective during times when financial decisions may feel most difficult. The right advisor is not only a resource for building wealth but also a partner in strengthening your long-term financial confidence.

That said, it's important to have realistic expectations. No one, no matter how experienced, can time the market consistently, eliminate all risk, or guarantee performance. The financial markets are inherently unpredictable, and even the best strategies will experience periods of volatility. What matters is working with an advisor who follows a disciplined, evidence-based approach. Ideally, someone who helps you balance risk and reward while staying focused on your short- and long-term goals. Instead of chasing short-term gains or reacting emotionally to market swings, a qualified advisor should help you build and maintain a portfolio that aligns with your financial objectives, time horizon, and comfort with risk. They should also help you understand the strategy they're using and provide education, transparency, and guidance so you can feel confident in the overall direction, the decisions being made, and how the capital markets are being used to serve your needs.

At our firm, we also believe everyone should have a comprehensive financial plan, because at the core of good financial planning is the discipline to stick to your strategy, looking at your total financial picture. Even when markets wobble, a financial plan helps you avoid emotion-driven decisions and ensures every move supports your short- and long-term needs. Market dips are inevitable, but with thoughtful planning and steady execution, they don't have to derail your progress. Is your goal to chase returns and react to headlines, or is it to build a financial future that supports your lifestyle, priorities, and legacy?

An experienced advisor first helps you identify your goals, needs, and priorities by looking at your entire financial picture, and then they keep you grounded, focused, and aligned. This can be especially important when fear or uncertainty creeps in. Real financial success is not about timing the market or chasing short-term gains. It is about creating an income plan you can rely on for life, keeping pace with the rising cost of living, being tax smart, considering legacy desires, and implementing sound strategies that move you toward your goals. Your financial plan and investment strategy should adapt when needed but remain rooted in long-term needs. In my view there is no better way to build this than with a professional who keeps their fingers on the pulse of your entire financial picture and the forces that can shape it.

Your Estate Attorney

Estate planning goes beyond wills and what happens after death. It's a process that provides protection, structure, and control while you're still alive, and because of that estate planning is best handled with the help of a skilled estate attorney. An attorney can help ensure your financial and personal plans reflect your wishes. This includes keeping foundational documents such as your will, trust, powers of attorney, healthcare directives, and beneficiary designations up to date and aligned with your intent. But estate planning is more than just paperwork. A good attorney also ensures your assets are properly titled, your plans are legally enforceable, and your loved ones are spared from unnecessary probate delays, avoidable taxes, and potential family conflict.

After the death of a spouse, an estate attorney's role is not just to adjust documents, but to help you navigate the complex transition from joint to individual ownership with insight and care. They guide you through questions you may not even know to ask, such as whether your assets are titled for maximum protection, whether your contingent beneficiaries are up to date, and whether new risks to your legacy have emerged now that you are managing it alone.

It's also important to be realistic about the process. Proper estate planning takes time, effort, and, yes, some financial investment. A thorough estate review isn't completed in a single short meeting. It often requires gathering documentation, providing account details, understanding family dynamics, and making thoughtful choices about how you want assets to be distributed and managed. Be prepared to answer personal questions, revisit old assumptions, and spend time communicating your true wishes.

The cost of creating or updating an estate plan can vary widely depending on complexity. It could be several thousand for comprehensive plans involving trusts, advanced tax strategies, or blended family dynamics. As I understand it, planning these days may cost $5,000 or more, although it can vary by state and attorney. However, the real cost comes from not doing it properly. That's because probate fees, unnecessary taxes, court battles, and unintended consequences can quickly and by far exceed the cost of good planning.

To make estate planning more affordable and accessible, a few advisory firms, ours included, now offer secure digital platforms that allow clients to create legally valid wills, trusts, healthcare directives, and powers of attorney online. These tools can accommodate a wide range of needs, including revocable and irrevocable trusts, without the time and expense often associated with traditional attorney-only models. For many individuals and families, they offer an efficient and reliable way to ensure their wishes are documented and enforceable. That said, not all online estate services offer the same level of legal oversight or customization. If you pursue self-directed estate planning, it's important to evaluate whether the platform you're using includes attorney review, complies with state-specific laws, and aligns with your overall planning goals.

Of course, in situations involving highly complex tax strategies, multi-generational wealth planning, or unique legal structures, working directly with an estate attorney may still be advisable. Estate planning is not one-size-fits-all, and the right approach depends on the complexity of your life, your goals, and your legacy.

This is not an area where you should rush or bargain hunt. Taking the time to do it right today gives you peace of mind and helps prevent problems that could surface later when they are hardest to fix. Estate planning is about building a structure that protects you, your loved ones, and everything you have worked so hard to create. It is not a single event but an ongoing part of your financial life that grows and adapts as you do. The right plan gives you confidence that your wishes will be honored, your family will be cared for, and your legacy will live on.

Your CPA or Tax Professional

Your tax picture changes dramatically in widowhood. You may move into a different tax bracket, your filing status will change, and you might trigger new taxes on Social Security benefits or Medicare premiums. Required minimum distributions (RMDs) may impact your taxable income differently. Every piece now fits together in a new and sometimes more complicated puzzle, including a range of diversified issues such as investment gains, property sales, Roth conversions, inherited assets, and more.

A qualified tax professional who understands your full financial picture is essential in helping you avoid unnecessary taxes, seize tax-planning opportunities, and protect your wealth over time. They can help you project future tax liabilities, plan the timing and amounts of IRA distributions, structure Roth conversions strategically, and think through the tax impact of gifts, inheritances, and charitable giving. They also help you navigate shifting state and federal tax laws that could materially affect your plans.

But it's not just about preparing tax returns at the end of the year. Your tax advisor is a critical part of your decision-making team when it comes to reviewing major financial moves before you make them. Decisions such as selling property, cashing out retirement accounts, exercising stock options, or gifting large sums can create permanent tax consequences. Ideally, your tax and financial advisor will work together as a collaborative team to help ensure that your financial moves are coordinated, strategic, and tax efficient.

Of course, this collaboration must be forward-looking. True tax planning happens *before* actions are taken, not after the fact. Unfortunately, and all too often, individuals act first and only involve their advisors afterward. This limits the options available and could lock in avoidable taxes. By proactively involving your advisors in key financial decisions, you give yourself the best chance to optimize your outcomes, preserve more of your wealth, and avoid costly mistakes.

Having a CPA or tax expert is not just for the wealthy. It is for anyone who wants to make the most of what they have built and avoid unnecessary surprises. As with the rest of your professional advisors, the value comes from foresight, not after-the-fact fixes. Good tax planning is proactive, not reactive. It is about understanding how today's choices shape tomorrow's opportunities. A skilled tax advisor looks beyond tax returns and helps you anticipate changes, identify strategies, and keep your financial life on track. While they may collaborate with your financial advisor and estate attorney, their role is distinct. They bring the tax lens that ensures your planning is efficient, practical, and aligned with your goals. With a professional team on your side, you are not just filing paperwork, you are taking control of your future.

Your Trusted Contact or Advocate

In addition to licensed professionals, when you are single it is wise to name someone as your trusted contact. This is someone who knows you personally and can recognize when something is not right. This could be an adult child, a sibling, or a close friend. Your trusted contact does not need legal authority or access to your money because they are not a decision-maker. But they are an important point of contact because they serve as a safeguard. By naming a trusted contact on your accounts, you give your advisor, attorney, bank or custodian permission to reach out if they notice signs of trouble, such as unusual withdrawals, erratic behavior, or decisions that do not align with your past patterns. The role is simple but vital.

A trusted contact acts as an early warning system. They help protect you from the risks of isolation, exploitation, or the early signs of cognitive decline that can too easily go unnoticed. Think of them as an extra layer of defense built on trust, familiarity, and care. Consequently, choosing a trusted contact thoughtfully is as important as choosing your professionals. You want someone who respects your independence, understands your values, and is willing to act in your best interest if concerns arise. You certainly don't want someone who would misuse their position or create conflict. It's a protective step that honors your autonomy while providing a strong safety net if life takes an unexpected turn.

CREATING A PERSONAL SAFETY SYSTEM

When your financial advisor, estate attorney, CPA, and trusted contact all work together you get far more than advice. You get protection. You build a line of defense between yourself and costly errors, legal blind spots, and bad actors. As challenges or questions arise you'll have a team that helps you stay steady, proactive, and prepared.

Even with the right team, however, the most important safeguard is you. The guidance of trusted professionals is invaluable, yet lasting protection also depends on the personal systems you put in place. These are the habits and boundaries that give you space to pause, think clearly, and act on your own terms.

One of the smartest moves you can make is giving yourself explicit permission to pause before making major decisions. In times of transition, pressure from others or from within yourself can lead to impulsive choices. Establishing simple personal policies ahead of time gives you a framework for when emotions run high. Think about where you are most vulnerable. Are you at risk of impulse spending? Do you tend to be too trusting of others? Do you often feel pressured to say yes? Do you procrastinate? Whatever your patterns, put guardrails in place now. This allows you to lean on a rational approach when you are clear-minded so you are protected before you ever find yourself in a vulnerable position.

It can also help to create a personal checklist or rulebook. Think of it as a self-imposed circuit breaker to prevent costly mistakes. Your list might include rules like:

- Sleep on any major purchase or commitment for at least 48 hours.
- No financial gifts, loans, or favors over $500 without a second review.
- Never sign legal or financial documents without discussing them first with your advisors.
- Pause and review if something feels rushed, confusing, or out of character.
- Do not delay important decisions beyond three days without taking one clear next step.

Keep in mind, these guidelines aren't about limiting your freedom. They're about protecting your independence and giving you the structure to move forward with confidence. When you have pre-set rules in place, you relieve yourself of the burden of making high-pressure calls in emotionally charged moments, but you also avoid ignoring important matters.

IF YOU'VE ALREADY MADE A MISTAKE: WHAT NOW?

Mistakes happen. Even smart, capable people make errors. Financial missteps, emotional decisions, or misplaced trust do not make you irresponsible. They are simply part of life. What matters most is not the mistake itself but how you respond to it. If you realize you have made a financial misstep, the first step is to pause, assess the situation, and not panic.

How significant is the damage?

- Is the mistake reversible?
- What options are still available?

Sometimes a quick correction is possible. Other times, it may require a longer recovery plan. Either way, the most important thing is to avoid letting fear, shame, or embarrassment cause further harm through rushed decisions or avoidance. If the situation involves suspected fraud, exploitation, or a transaction you don't fully understand, involve professionals immediately. Reach out to your financial advisor, CPA, estate attorney, or custodian. It's far easier to contain and correct issues when they are addressed early rather than ignored out of fear or uncertainty.

Above all, approach yourself with grace. Nearly everyone navigating new financial waters has made decisions they wish they could undo. Strength isn't pretending mistakes never happen. It is recognizing missteps, taking action to address them, and turning the experience into fuel for better, stronger decision-making going forward.

STRENGTH ISN'T JUST MOVING FORWARD—IT'S STANDING GUARD

It's easy to believe that strength means simply pushing forward. But real strength that builds and preserves a lasting legacy is just as much about vigilance as it is about momentum.

You are the steward now. And with that role comes the right and the responsibility to protect what you have earned, what you have built, and what you envision for the future. You are allowed to pause, to ask questions, and to require accountability. You are allowed to say no. Strength is not about pretending nothing can reach you. It is about standing watch, standing tall, and making deliberate choices that serve your best interest without apology.

CHAPTER EIGHT

From What Was to What Will Be

Rebuilding Retirement after Loss

Time doesn't return what was.
It offers what could be.

Life did not unfold as you planned, and adjusting to loss is never easy. But you can still move forward with resolve. Rebuilding your life in retirement is not about starting over. It is about creating a future that reflects your values, responds to your new reality, and aligns with your goals. Your life may not look as you once envisioned, yet that does not prevent you from shaping a new vision. Imagining what comes next is not indulgence. It is resilience.

Take an honest look at where you are today and give yourself permission to move forward. Begin with steady steps. Reassess your goals, reevaluate income needs, adjust investments, and refine your estate and financial plans. These are the building blocks of a secure foundation. In time, strength will return, and with each decision, confidence will grow.

When Jenny lost Brian unexpectedly on that summer evening, she spent months in a fog. She could not imagine retiring without him and resisted the idea of life without his companionship. Yet over time she took small steps to re-engage. Slowly she got back out in the world and pursued hobbies, built new friendships, and found fulfillment through volunteering. She updated her financial plan and engaged a new team of professionals, which gave her the confidence to move forward. She also discovered joy in being a grandmother, finding comfort and purpose in the time she spent with her grandchildren. Their presence reminded her that while life had changed, love and connection were still very much a part of her future. Jenny's life was never the same without Brian, of course, but she carried him with her as she reshaped her future. By persevering, she created a retirement full of meaning, connection, and even joy.

It may feel overwhelming to picture a future without your spouse. But ask yourself what they would have wanted for you. If the roles were reversed, would you have wished them to remain in grief, or to carry on with peace and purpose? That same permission to live belongs to you now.

What matters is not whether the path will be easy, but how you choose to walk it. Walk it with resolve, knowing strength also lives within you. The journey ahead is yours to shape. Life's possibilities extend beyond what was lost toward what still can be. Loss is part of your story, but not the whole story. The chapters ahead are yours to write, guided by your experience but not defined by it.

FOR THOSE OF FAITH, LET THAT BE YOUR BEACON

If you are a person of faith, you may find solace in the belief that life continues beyond this world and that reunion with loved ones awaits. That assurance can serve as an anchor as you move forward. Faith reminds us that love is not confined to time and that relationships built in this life are not erased by death. In moments of grief, let that belief steady your heart and provide the reassurance that separation is not the end of the story.

Allow that conviction to give you strength. Let it guide you to live with purpose, compassion, and resolve, knowing your spouse remains with you in spirit. Honor the bond you shared by making this time meaningful. Every day you move forward with intention is both a tribute to the love that endures and a preparation for the moment when you are reunited.

WHEN FAITH FEELS DISTANT: FINDING HOPE ANYWAY

If you struggle with faith, you are not alone. Grief can shake even the strongest beliefs and leave you questioning what once felt certain. Anger, doubt, or a sense of abandonment are natural responses to loss. Wrestling with questions of why and what comes next does not make you weak. It is a human response to profound change.

Even without full certainty, hope still matters. It is present in the decision to keep moving forward when answers are unclear. It lives in how we honor the love we knew, the memories we carry, and the people who shaped our lives. Strength is not about unshakable faith. It is about continuing to care, to build, and to engage in life even when belief feels distant.

Your ability to move forward does not depend on having every spiritual question resolved. It comes from small, deliberate steps. It's about getting up, participating in life, reaching out, and carrying forward what mattered most in your relationship. Hope can be found in many forms such as a quiet prayer, in a meaningful memory, in the smile of a grandchild, or in the promise of a new day.

You do not need perfect faith to create a meaningful future. You need only the willingness to keep living, to keep seeking, and to accept that even after loss, life can still hold new joys, new purposes, and new beginnings.

WHEN FAITH ISN'T PART OF YOUR STORY: FINDING STRENGTH IN WHAT REMAINS

If you do not believe in God or in life beyond this world, loss can feel especially final. Accepting death as an ending is painful. The absence of your spouse is real, and it is natural to feel the weight of it. Wondering how you will carry on in a life that feels unfamiliar is expected.

Yet even in that absence, much remains. The love you shared, the memories you hold, and the values you carry forward are not erased. Moving ahead does not diminish what was lost. Moving forward preserves and honors it.

The life you have now is where those lessons and influences continue. Even without belief in eternity, the impact of one life on another endures. You do not need to believe in forever to see the importance of today. The choices you make, the relationships you build, and the way you live are proof that meaning and purpose remain possible.

REDEFINING PURPOSE: FINDING NEW CONNECTIONS, NEW HOBBIES, AND NEW SOURCES OF STRENGTH

Retirement still offers possibilities. Give yourself the freedom to explore. Take a pottery class, learn a new language, plan a trip, or volunteer your time where it is needed. The limits are the ones you place on yourself.

Community also plays an important role. Reach outward and build friendships and connections that fit the person you are becoming. Local groups, classes, clubs, and social organizations can help you meet others with similar interests. You may not know exactly what will inspire you, but with openness and steady effort you can move toward new connections and opportunities.

Finding New Hobbies and Interests

Retirement provides the time and flexibility to explore new activities. Think about the interests you once set aside because of work or family, or areas you've never had the chance to try. Curiosity, even in small doses, can open the door to a more engaging and fulfilling retirement.

Consider skills or hobbies you once wished to pursue but didn't. It could be painting, woodworking, cooking, gardening, writing, photography, sailing, or learning an instrument. You may also want to explore physical activities such as pickleball, bowling, or simply getting back into the gym. Choose what feels authentic to you today.

If you are unsure where to begin, start small. Attend a lecture, visit a museum, take a short class, or explore a new subject through a book or online video. Experimentation is progress. Small efforts, taken consistently, can grow into lasting interests and meaningful pursuits.

How to Find Local Activities and Connections

- Check your town's Senior Center or Community Center. Most cities and towns have a senior center that organizes events, classes, group outings, and volunteer opportunities.

- Look for classes at local colleges or community education programs. Many schools offer adult enrichment classes in art, music, writing, fitness, technology, and cooking—often at low cost.

Category	Examples
Learning & Exploration	Community college classes, art workshops, photography courses, book clubs, senior centers or recreational centers
Fitness & Outdoor Activities	Walking groups, hiking clubs, yoga, tai chi, pickleball leagues
Creative Pursuits	Painting, woodworking, knitting, pottery, gardening, creative writing
Volunteering	Animal shelters, food banks, hospital programs, tutoring, local museums, church
Travel & Adventure	Group travel clubs, day trips, river cruises, solo travel meetups
Social Engagement	Wine tastings, cooking classes, dance classes, social meetups, lifelong learning groups
Faith & Spirituality	Faith-based study groups, interfaith service projects, spiritual retreats
Technology & Innovation	Tech workshops, genealogy research, virtual reality travel experiences
Music & Performing Arts	Choirs, theater groups, concert attendance, musical instrument lessons
Health & Wellness	Meditation groups, nutrition classes, senior fitness centers, spa retreats

- Visit your local library. Libraries host free workshops, book clubs, guest lectures, and social meetups geared toward adults.
- Use online platforms like Meetup and Eventbrite. Search for local gatherings by hobby, such as hiking groups, painting nights, language classes, or travel meetups.
- Join faith-based groups or volunteer organizations. Many churches, synagogues, and community charities host regular social activities open to anyone looking to connect.

- Sign up for fitness classes or clubs. Fitness centers, yoga studios, and even walking clubs offer ways to stay active and meet new people.
- Explore hobby shops and specialty stores. Craft stores, garden centers, music store, and cooking stores often offer workshops or hands-on classes where you can meet others with similar interests.
- Check local newspapers and magazines. Community calendars often highlight events, fairs, farmers markets, concerts, and local happenings.
- Don't be afraid to try something new. Even if it feels outside your comfort zone, attending an event just once can open the door to new friendships and activities.

Reaching Out to Your Community

Your community can play a central role in shaping a fulfilling retirement. Building new friendships and connections is often one of the most valuable parts of this stage of life. Many retirees are looking for new circles of support and shared interests, and opportunities are everywhere. Walking groups, art classes, volunteer programs, and local travel clubs all provide ways to meet people and create meaningful relationships. You don't need to start with major commitments. Simply attending a class, a community event, or a day trip can open the door to connections that develop naturally over time. Community centers, libraries, senior programs, lifelong learning courses, nonprofit organizations, and faith communities often provide accessible and welcoming opportunities to engage.

Building new connections is not about replacing your past life or filling every gap at once. It is about taking manageable steps toward new networks that reflect who you are today. The first step is often the hardest, but each one that follows makes the process easier.

And because grief does not follow a set timeline, having support systems in place is especially important. Options include:

- Grief counseling, either individual or group-based. Many communities have licensed counselors specializing in bereavement.
- National organizations like GriefShare and The Compassionate Friends offer local and virtual support groups.
- Widow support groups, both in-person and online, can provide understanding and practical advice.
- Therapy apps and virtual mental health services if attending in-person is difficult or uncomfortable.

Remember, you are not meant to rebuild in isolation. There are people and communities ready to support you. And if you are reluctant, remember seeking support is not a sign of weakness. On the contrary, it is a mark of wisdom, courage, and self-respect.

TRAVELING SOLO AFTER LOSS: YOUR JOURNEY, YOUR TERMS

Travel often tops the list of retirement goals. It represents freedom, discovery, and the chance to experience the world beyond your day-to-day life. But we often hear single clients express reluctance because they feel they need a travel companion. If you once imagined seeing new places with your spouse, traveling on your own is bound to feel uncomfortable, but it can also be very rewarding.

Take Ruth, for example. She was a long-time client who didn't see her retirement as a time to slow down. She saw it as a time to enjoy a life she had dreamed about. And, as with many, one of her top goals was travel. She had a long list of places she wanted to visit. Even though she was single, she didn't let the fact that she was doing it on her own slow her down for one second.

Over the course of about ten years, Ruth traveled to some of the most breathtaking and exotic locations around the globe, from Cambodia to Thailand, from the Amazon rainforest to Iceland. She embraced adventure, new experiences, and new connections she made along the way.

What made Ruth's journey even more fulfilling was how she approached it. She found a travel group that fit her. She traveled with a company geared toward curious, independent-minded single adults. Over time, the other travelers and guides became more than just people she met on trips. They became a community, a network of familiar faces who shared her passion for discovery. Sadly, Ruth passed away at the age of 78. She had never married or had children, but she lived her retirement to its fullest. Her story, I think, is a powerful reminder that retirement is an open invitation to shape a new phase of life, regardless of your marital or family status. Ruth didn't just check destinations off a list. She built a rich tapestry of experiences, friendships, and memories all on her own terms.

What I admired most about Ruth was her vibrant spirit, her hunger to learn, and her willingness to say *yes* to the world. She found connection and community by doing something she loved even though she didn't have a travel partner. She turned her quest for adventure into a way of life.

And she wasn't the only one.

Laura, another client, loves to travel the world. At 83, she spent an entire month exploring Morocco all on her own. With no family or friends accompanying her, her determination to experience something new took her across continents. Whether you are a few towns away or several countries away, these journeys prove that retirement as a single person is not the end of discovery.

Life as a widow or widower isn't about giving up on dreams. It's about reclaiming them in your own way, on your own timeline, and with a renewed sense of purpose. The world is still waiting for you. There are still cities to explore, cultures to experience, sunsets to witness, and memories to create. If travel is on your list, make it happen.

Howard found his own way to keep traveling with the person he loved. After losing his wife, Marilyn, to a long illness, he made a promise to her that he would keep seeing the world and bring her with him in spirit. Wherever he goes he carries a photo of Marilyn. He often asks strangers if they would take a picture of him and his wife. People look around, searching for her, and when he pulls out the photo and explains that she passed away from cancer but always dreamed of touring the Vatican or Edinburgh Castle or wherever he was visiting, the moment changes. People lean in. They listen. They want to hear more.

Howard often ends up sharing lunch, a cup of coffee, or even an evening with new friends he meets this way. He gets to share his memories about how he and Marilyn raised four children and talks about his life with her on their small farm. Whether he's standing in front of the Eiffel Tower, cruising the canals of Venice, or sitting in a pub in Ireland, he always has Marilyn, and her photo, by his side. He even shares his adventures on social media, where over time he's built quite a following. People are inspired by his will to carry on and love following how he honors her memory, even as he continues to move forward and creates new memories of his own.

Practical Tips for Traveling as a Single Retiree

If you want to explore the world like many others, don't let being single stop you. Start with places that inspire you. Whether it's a national park, a seaside village, or a city you always wanted to see, let curiosity lead you forward. Often, traveling alone invites company. People are friendly and welcoming, curious about where you are from, and eager to hear your story.

Want some tips and tricks for meeting people while traveling solo? Sit at the bar instead of a table when dining out. Casual conversation happens more naturally at a bar, even if you just eat. Or choose an outdoor café where you can people watch. Join small group tours or classes that match your interests while traveling. Attend a cooking class, photography tour, or art workshop. You might meet someone whose company you would enjoy over dinner. Staying in boutique hotels, bed and breakfasts, or inns that host community breakfasts or social hours provides for easy conversation. Simply by being open, offering a smile, a question about directions, or a compliment can open doors to wonderful connections you might not have planned for.

I once hosted a blind man for a business speaking engagement and spent several days with him. I was struck by the fact that he didn't use a walking stick or a guide dog, so I asked him why. He smiled and said, "People are far more interesting than a stick." And he went on to tell me about the amazing people he had met on the streets. His blindness gave him a reason to reach out to others. Of course, he had to ask for help to cross the street or open a door. His story stayed with me because he had turned what many see as a limitation into an invitation, using his vulnerability to create moments of genuine human connection.

Exploring solo-friendly group travel is also a great way to feel connected while pursuing your adventures. Companies like Road Scholar, Overseas Adventure Travel, and Stitch design trips specifically for independent adults, taking the logistics and guesswork out of the experience. Choose experiences that match your interests. Whether it's wine tasting, art history tours, outdoor adventures, or cultural exchanges, travel is an opportunity to deepen your passions. And embrace flexibility. One of the best parts of traveling solo is the freedom to set your own pace, change plans on a whim, or discover unexpected opportunities along the way.

Of course, stay safe while staying connected. Smart solo travel means booking reputable accommodations and, obviously, staying aware of your surroundings. It's also smart to share your itinerary with family or friends. But don't let your loss limit you. Create your own travel traditions. Whether it's taking a special photo at each destination, trying a local dish, or writing a short reflection after each trip, you're building something new and meaningful.

At first traveling alone might feel uncomfortable or even lonely. It's easy to assume that being in a bustling city, surrounded by people, will automatically make you feel connected, but if you focus on what's missing, you can end up feeling more isolated sitting at busy restaurant than you did back at home. However, these are normal feelings, especially when you first venture out on your own. You might miss your spouse's voice beside you, his or her shared laughter over a crooked street sign, or the ease of having someone to enjoy the small moments with.

The key is to recognize those lonely moments for what they are. They are a natural part of adjusting to a new kind of life. But they are not a reason to retreat. I often lament that growth doesn't happen inside your comfort zone, and that certainly holds true here. You can't expect to step into a new life after years or even decades of walking side by side with someone without feeling at least a bit unsettled.

In fact, some clients have told me they are downright scared to travel alone. Others have been traveling solo for decades. With time, familiarity comes, so give it a chance. I remember when I first became single after 20 years in marriage. I went out to eat at a café while on a business trip in Boston and felt acutely aware of myself sitting alone. I noticed the other tables around me. People were laughing, talking, sharing stories, and I felt the absence of my former spouse and became deeply self-conscious. Then I noticed the way the light struck an old stone building across the street. It was so beautiful that I was mesmerized. Then I noticed a young couple at a nearby table. They were leaning toward each other, hands lightly touching, eyes locked with the attentive curiosity of a first date, and suddenly I realized my thoughts weren't on being alone, but on the quiet joy I felt for them. Eventually, I learned to savor a meal out and stopped worrying about who might be watching me dine alone. Instead, I began to appreciate the flavors of the meal, the energy around me, and the simple pleasure of being present.

You may notice a bird you've never seen before or enjoy the clouds in the sky. Rather than dwelling on who is not there to share it, the more you go out, the more you will feel a small spark of wonder at the world still unfolding around you. Each time you remain open, even when it feels uncomfortable, you strengthen your spirit. Over time those small shifts add up to a life that feels connected again to beauty and to possibility.

If you want to travel, do it. Don't let loss keep you from new experiences. I recently spent a week on a land tour in Alaska and made numerous friends. At first, conversations were quiet and tentative, but after several days together the motorcoach was filled with laughter and easy conversation. The more you step out, the sooner the discomfort fades, and in its place grows a quiet confidence. By opening yourself to the world, even as a widow or widower, you can still find happiness, wonder, and new friendships wherever you go.

Here are some additional online resources to consider as well:

Resource Name	Purpose	Website Address
Road Scholar	Educational travel programs for older adults, including solo traveler trips.	roadscholar.org
Meetup	Find local groups by interests such as hiking, book clubs, travel, and more.	meetup.com
Stitch	Social community just for adults 50+, including travel, activities, companionship.	stitch.net
Solo Traveler	Resource hub for solo travelers, including seniors, with trips, tips, and groups.	solotravelerworld.com
AARP Community Connections	Volunteer opportunities, virtual events, and activity finders.	aarpcommunity connections.org
Amtrak Vacations	Group train travel packages, some designed for solo or senior travelers.	amtrakvacations.com
Senior Planet from AARP	Free online classes, lectures, and events about hobbies, technology, and fitness.	seniorplanet.org
TravelAwaits	Articles, travel deals, and destination ideas for travelers over 50.	travelawaits.com
National Parks Senior Pass	Affordable access to National Parks for retirees who love nature and adventure.	nps.gov/planyourvisit/ senior-pass-changes.htm
YMCA	Many local YMCAs offer senior fitness, art, and social engagement programs.	ymca.org/find-your-y

FINDING LOVE AGAIN, COMPANIONSHIP, AND PROTECTING YOUR FUTURE

The love you shared with your spouse will always remain part of your story. It shaped who you are and continues through the memories, meaning, and family you built together. Nothing—not time, distance, or even new relationships—takes that away. For some, the idea of loving again feels impossible. But for others, the possibility develops through a friendship, a conversation, or a chance encounter. It is completely acceptable to welcome that possibility if and when you are ready.

There is no timeline and no single "right" answer. Whether companionship becomes friendship, partnership, or marriage, your path is your own. And it is natural to hold the past close while also opening yourself to the future.

We have had clients who never pursued love again, and others who remarried, even in their 80s. Kelly and Eleanor were two of my favorites. Both had lost their spouses after long, happy marriages. They met at church. Neither was expecting to fall in love again, but they did. They married and shared 19 years together before Kelly passed at the age of 99. At his funeral, Eleanor fussed over him one last time, straightening his bow tie and making sure he looked just as she wanted to remember him. Their story is a reminder that joy can return, sometimes when it is least expected.

Bruce's wife passed away after a long battle with cancer. He was devoted to her through every appointment, treatment, and long day of caregiving. Less than a year after her passing, Bruce called me with a mix of excitement and nerves to share that he was remarrying. He had met someone in his bowling league. At 78, as he put it, "I don't know how long I have, but I'd rather share it with someone than be alone." He admitted to feeling a little guilty, but his story shows that there are no rules or timelines. The desire for love and connection remains important at any age.

It is also common to worry about judgment, whether from others or from yourself. Family members or adult children may not understand, and you may question whether seeking happiness again diminishes the love you shared with your spouse. But your life is your own. Choosing to remarry is not a betrayal. It is an extension of the love and vitality that shaped your past. While pursuing a new relationship is always a choice, doing so should be free from guilt and guided by your own readiness.

Harry was a devoted father, a dedicated grandfather, and a deeply loyal husband. After the loss of his wife, he spent several years trying to adjust to life on his own. He stayed in the same home they had shared and slowly learned to adapt to the quieter rhythms of life. He often spoke of Marla with deep affection, and it was clear that her absence left a lasting ache. But his days were lonely, and he told me that it often felt as though life was simply passing him by. He watched television, ran errands, and made himself dinner, but he said he felt like he was just going through the motions. He admitted he was struggling to find hobbies that truly interested him or people his own age with whom he felt a genuine connection.

Over time, Harry began to venture out more, meeting other retirees. Gradually he found himself part of a new circle, including a woman he took a liking to. At first he referred to her simply as his "lady friend," making it very clear she was a companion, not a replacement for the wife he had loved so dearly. But as time went on, Harry grew more comfortable and open, eventually calling her his girlfriend.

He always told me he would never remarry. He said his vow to his late wife was something he intended to carry for the rest of his life. But his lady friend brought a bounce back into his step and helped him rediscover happiness in ways he thought were lost forever. They go out on dates, travel together, share time with each other's families. She opened his world to new people, new experiences, and helped him find happiness in his heart again. It wasn't about replacing the love he had lost, but adding to the life he still had left to live.

Whether or not you decide to pursue love or companionship is a deeply personal choice and there is no formula to determine the right time or the right way. But if you do open yourself to it, preparation matters. Protecting yourself financially, legally, and emotionally is not about distrust. It is about safeguarding what you have built, protecting your family, and ensuring that what comes next is secure and fulfilling. Moving forward with both an open heart and open eyes allows you to honor your past while building a future that is both safe and meaningful.

How a New Relationship Changes Your Financial Picture

When love, companionship, or deep friendship comes into your life again after loss, it can feel like a sunrise after a long dark night. Whether it arrives gently or catches you by surprise, it brings new energy, new possibilities, and often a renewed sense of purpose. It reminds you that life is still unfolding, that happiness is still possible, and that your story is not yet complete.

But while the emotional spark of a new relationship can be uplifting, it's important to recognize that even the most beautiful new beginning brings practical realities with it. Love does not erase the financial structures and responsibilities you spent years carefully building. In fact, it often complicates them and deserves thoughtful attention.

A new relationship changes your financial picture simply because it changes how you live. Even if you intend to "keep things separate," life rarely remains entirely separate for long.

Decisions get taken together—from how and where you travel, to how you spend money, to where you live and even what health care looks like as you age. Emotions naturally blend with daily living, and daily living naturally blends into financial choices.

Sharing your life with someone again, whether through dating, living together, or marriage, changes your day-to-day expenses. It may also affect your eligibility for government benefits. It might expose your estate or assets to new legal risks. It can even subtly shift how your children or grandchildren perceive your financial intentions, sometimes creating misunderstandings. None of this means you should hold back from embracing companionship. If you are ready and are fortunate enough to find someone whose presence adds to your happiness, that is something to celebrate. But it is wise to step into this carefully.

Too often people assume that new relationships will have no real impact because they plan to "keep things casual" or "not get married." But finances, taxes, Social Security, Medicare premiums, legal standing, and family expectations don't always distinguish between formal marriage and informal life partnerships. Simply sharing an address, paying bills together, or being named as an emergency contact can create assumptions, socially and legally, that entangle your financial life with someone else's in ways you didn't plan. And while love is often spontaneous, financial security is not.

Financial security must be intentional. You spent decades building stability. You safeguarded your family's future. You made careful decisions, sometimes under the hardest circumstances, to protect your well-being. That same care deserves to accompany you into a new relationship. This reality is not meant to dim your happiness, but to protect it.

When a new relationship begins, it is natural to enjoy the bond and the companionship it brings, but it also affects practical matters. Household spending often shifts when someone new shares your life. Retirement income may be stretched differently. As the relationship deepens, health care decisions and long-term planning may need to be reconsidered. And if you have adult children, your choices can raise questions about inheritances, family property, and caregiving responsibilities, even if that was never your intent.

Again, these are not reasons to pull away from love or to fear connection, but they are reasons to be wise and deliberate. You are not who you were in your twenties or thirties, stepping into love with nothing but a suitcase and a smile. You are someone who has lived a full life already. You are someone with assets, responsibilities, and a family history to honor. Protecting yourself financially, legally, and emotionally is not a betrayal of your new relationship. It is a way to ensure that your happiness is built on a strong, secure foundation. It allows you to enjoy this journey without fear, hesitation, or future regrets.

As you explore companionship, dating, or marriage again, the best gift you can give yourself is to stay grounded. Celebrate the emotions that come with new beginnings, but also take time early on to understand how this relationship fits into the larger structure of your financial life. Not every decision must be made immediately, of course, but knowing that financial implications exist, and planning thoughtfully, can prevent misunderstandings later.

You deserve to live with joy and security. You deserve to protect the life you have built and the people you love, and this includes those who walked before and those who may walk with you now. That is why thoughtfulness before decisions are tangled with emotion is not a limitation. It is an act of strength, wisdom, and love. New relationships can affect key financial areas, from Social Security benefits to tax consequences, estate planning, and financial management. Whether you choose to formally remarry, live together, or simply travel the road of life with a companion, you deserve to move forward fully informed, fully protected, and fully alive to the possibilities still ahead.

Social Security Benefits and Remarriage Rules

As you consider the possibility of remarriage, it is important to understand how this decision affects Social Security survivor benefits. The rules are specific, and remarriage can significantly alter your eligibility and long-term financial picture if these are not carefully reviewed.

If you remarry before age 60, you forfeit your right to collect Social Security survivor benefits based on your late spouse's earnings record. In essence, Social Security views your remarriage before 60 as establishing a new marital relationship, and therefore, the tie to your deceased spouse's benefit is severed. This can come as an unpleasant surprise if not properly planned for, particularly if the survivor benefit you were entitled to would have been larger than the benefit you could claim on your new spouse's record, or your own.

However, if you remarry at age 60 or older, you are generally allowed to retain your survivor benefits. In other words, the Social Security Administration continues to recognize your eligibility based on your deceased spouse's work history even though you have remarried. This is a crucial distinction and can offer you greater flexibility. You could remarry without jeopardizing the survivor benefit, and later, if advantageous, you could switch to benefits on your own record or your new spouse's record if they would yield a higher amount. But timing is everything. A remarriage just weeks before turning 60 could have lifelong consequences for your financial security, while waiting until after your 60th birthday preserves your options.

Beyond the remarriage rules, it's also important to think about how your decision to claim survivor benefits fits into your broader Social Security filing strategy. When you are entitled to multiple benefits, such as your own retirement benefit and a survivor benefit, you may have options about which one to take first and when. Filing for the survivor benefit early can allow your own retirement benefit to continue growing if you defer it, earning delayed retirement credits up to age 70. This flexibility can be a critical part of maximizing lifetime Social Security income, but only if you are aware of your rights and the timelines involved.

It is important to keep in mind that in order to qualify for Social Security spousal benefits, you typically need to have been married for at least one full year before you can claim based on your spouse's work record. If you are married at the time of filing, you will receive whichever is greater—the spousal benefit or your own benefit. Survivor benefits work differently. You can claim a survivor benefit as early as age 60, or age 50 if you are disabled, and later switch to your own retirement benefit at age 70 to take advantage of delayed retirement credits. However, if you remarry before age 60 (or 50 if disabled), you will generally lose eligibility for survivor benefits from your late spouse. But, if you remarry at age 60 or later, you may continue to receive survivor benefits.

A new marriage can unintentionally change your eligibility and affect the benefits you've earned. On the other hand, if you're collecting benefits based on your own record, remarriage isn't an issue. Your benefits stay exactly the same.

If you remarry before age 60, you will lose eligibility for survivor benefits while that marriage is in effect. However, if the remarriage ends, whether by divorce, annulment, or death, you regain eligibility to file for survivor benefits under your deceased first spouse's record. It's complicated, which is why knowing the rules ahead of time helps you make informed decisions that protect your financial future while honoring your personal journey. Ultimately, understanding the remarriage rules ensures that you do not accidentally close doors you might have wanted to leave open. So whether or not remarriage is part of your future, knowing how timing affects your benefits allows you to move forward with greater confidence and financial security.

Should You Legally Marry, Live Together, or Stay Separate?

Choosing whether to legally marry, live together, or maintain separate households later in life is not simply a matter of personal preference. The decision can directly affect your taxes, your retirement income, your healthcare costs, your estate plans, and your financial independence. In this stage of life, it's critical to weigh the emotional rewards against the practical realities, so that whatever path you choose, it fully supports both your heart and your future security.

Taxes are one of the first areas where marriage can have a surprising financial impact. While married couples often benefit from a larger standard deduction and wider tax brackets, two older adults, especially if both are drawing Social Security, pensions, investment income, or required minimum distributions, may still find that combining their incomes results in a higher overall tax burden. Although the brackets are generally more favorable for married couples filing jointly, retirement income can add up quickly. That additional income can reduce deductions, expose more Social Security benefits to taxation, and increase the amount of income taxed at higher marginal rates. The result is that marriage may lead to a larger federal tax bill than if each partner had remained single, and that is a reality that many do not anticipate when planning the next chapter of their lives.

Beyond taxes, marriage can also affect your healthcare costs. Although Medicare's IRMAA thresholds are doubled for married couples, combining two income streams can still push you into surcharge territory faster than expected. Higher income means higher Medicare Part B and Part D premiums for each spouse individually, adding thousands of dollars a year in healthcare costs. This so-called 'marriage penalty' is especially important if both partners have strong retirement incomes. It can also create complications if you have been diligent about tax planning and your new spouse has not, since their lack of preparation can directly impact the costs you face together.

In short, marriage in retirement doesn't always deliver the financial savings people expect. While the emotional benefits of marriage are very real, it's important to have a clear-eyed conversation about how taxes, Medicare premiums, and future healthcare expenses could change before making any legal commitment.

Pensions and survivor benefits tied to a deceased spouse's work record may be lost upon remarriage, depending on the specific rules of the pension plan. Some plans terminate survivor benefits the moment you remarry, even if you remarry after age 60. Consequently, it's critical to review any pension paperwork or call the plan administrator before making a decision.

While no one plans on needing Medicaid, this may be another critical area to consider. Medicaid eligibility for long-term care assistance is based on total household income and assets, not how you file your taxes or whether you have a prenuptial agreement. If you remarry, your new spouse's financial resources are considered part of your eligibility calculation, even if you maintain completely separate accounts. Prenuptial agreements do not shield assets from Medicaid calculations, nor does filing taxes separately. That means remarrying someone with significant resources could disqualify you from receiving Medicaid benefits if you later require nursing home care, forcing you to deplete your combined resources first. Or it can go the other way around. Your assets could end up being used for their care before Medicaid steps in, which could impact your financial security if you remain healthy and reduce what is ultimately available to your heirs. Understanding these rules ahead of time is essential to protect your long-term future.

If Medicaid eligibility is a concern, there are legal strategies that may help protect assets after marriage, but they require careful planning and professional guidance. For instance, certain irrevocable trusts may be used in some situations, though they come with strict rules, lookback periods, and state-specific limitations. Techniques like spousal refusal (available in some states) or Medicaid-compliant annuities can sometimes preserve resources for the healthy spouse while still qualifying the other for benefits. These strategies are highly technical, complex, and vary widely depending on state laws. If you're considering remarriage and want to protect long-term care options, it's wise to consult with an experienced elder law attorney or qualified financial advisor before making any financial or legal decisions.

Estate planning can also become tangled. If you marry without a prenuptial agreement, your new spouse may have automatic rights under state law to inherit a portion of your estate, even if you intended to leave everything to your children or other beneficiaries. In many states, a surviving spouse is legally entitled to an "elective share" of the estate. This means that regardless of what your will or trust says, your spouse can claim a portion of your assets, often one-third to one-half, depending on state law. While this rule is designed to prevent someone from being completely disinherited, it can create conflict among heirs and disrupt your original wishes if plans are not carefully made.

A close friend of mine remarried later in life. Her husband, a widower, had significantly greater financial means and had long planned to leave his estate to his three adult children. While understandable, that structure left her financially exposed, especially because he hoped she would retire far earlier than she had planned, putting her own long-term security at risk. With professional guidance, they created a trust that provided her with steady income and the right to remain in their home if something happened to him, while preserving the remaining assets for his children. Over time, as their marriage deepened, they chose to revise their plan. After fifteen years together, they redrafted the trust so she would receive half of the estate, and they went on to enjoy a fulfilling retirement with a plan that reflected both protection and partnership.

As you can see, when you move forward after widowhood, estate planning becomes more important than ever, and yet it can also get more complicated. Remarriage, companionship, or simply the passage of time can change your goals and the people you want to protect. If you don't update your estate plan with care, your assets may end up in the wrong hands, create conflict among loved ones, or leave your new partner vulnerable in ways you never intended.

It's a common misconception that keeping your assets separate after remarriage automatically protects them. While it's true that property you bring into a marriage is generally considered separate property, you must understand that you cannot commingle any accounts or assets by adding your spouse's name, using joint accounts, or blending funds. And, to the extent that you keep your accounts and assets separate, that protection only applies during your lifetime. Upon your death, most states give surviving spouses the right to claim an elective share of your estate, even if the assets were entirely separate.

While elective share rules vary by state, the general trend across the country is to allow surviving spouses to claim a share of both probate and non-probate assets, and that includes living trusts, which means your new spouse could be legally entitled to a portion of your separate property, thereby overriding your wishes and reducing what you intended to leave to your children, grandchildren, or other heirs.

Many people assume that placing their assets in a separate living trust will automatically protect those assets from a new spouse's inheritance rights after remarriage, but that's not the case. A revocable living trust is still considered your personal property during your lifetime because you maintain full control over it. That means the assets inside the trust can still be subject to a surviving spouse's elective share claim under state law, even if the trust says otherwise. Therefore, simply having a trust does not override your new spouse's legal right to claim a portion of your estate *unless you take further steps,* such as creating a prenuptial agreement that waives those rights.

In short, without careful planning, a remarriage could entitle your new spouse to a significant share of your trust assets upon your death, reducing what ultimately passes to your intended heirs. Protecting your estate requires more than setting up a trust. It requires making sure the trust, your marriage plans, and your broader estate documents all work together with a clear understanding of how remarriage changes the legal landscape.

Also, having a will alone does not prevent this. To fully protect your estate plan and honor your original intentions, you may need to create a prenuptial agreement, update or establish living trusts, and work with an estate planning attorney and advisory team who understand the complex rules around remarriage. Otherwise, even carefully kept separate property can be pulled into unintended legal claims after you're gone.

Finally, do not rely on default state laws to handle your estate if something happens to you. Without a will or proper planning, state laws such as intestacy rules, elective share provisions, or community property statutes will determine how your assets are divided. Many people mistakenly believe that everything will just go to their children or their new partner automatically. In reality, if you marry again without updating your estate plan, your new spouse may have rights to a significant share of your estate, even if your intent was to leave most of it to your children or grandchildren. Your state may divide assets in ways that look very different from what you intended.

Take control proactively. That means before you remarry (or even if you're simply entering into a committed long-term relationship) sit down with an estate planning attorney. Update key documents like your will, living trusts, powers of attorney, healthcare directives, and beneficiary designations to reflect your situation. Understanding how a prenuptial agreement clearly spells out how assets will be handled in life and after death can be of value. A prenuptial agreement is signed before marriage and can outline how property, retirement accounts, brokerage assets, and real estate will be divided (and protected) in the event of death or divorce. So the more prepared you are in advance, the better you can protect both yourself and those you love.

If you're already remarried and realize you need to address these issues, a postnuptial agreement may be an option. Like a prenuptial agreement, it can outline how property, retirement accounts, and other assets will be treated in life and at death, but it is signed after the marriage has taken place. A well-crafted postnup can bring clarity, protect children from prior relationships, and reduce the potential for conflict down the road. That said, a postnup is not always as strong as a prenup. Because it is signed after marriage, courts may scrutinize it more closely to ensure that both parties entered into it voluntarily, with full disclosure, and without coercion. In some states, postnups are harder to enforce or may even be limited in scope. A prenup, on the other hand, is generally more straightforward and less vulnerable to challenge since it is executed before legal marital rights attach.

Living Together—Domestic Partnership

If you choose to live together without marrying, it's important to know that domestic partnership laws vary widely. In most cases, unmarried partners have no automatic inheritance rights, which means without proper documents in place, your partner could be left with no legal authority or financial security if something happens to you. For example, in a medical crisis, your partner may have no legal right to make decisions for you unless you have executed a healthcare directive or power of attorney, leaving those choices in the hands of family members instead. If the property is titled in only one partner's name, the surviving partner may have no right to remain there, and children or relatives of the deceased partner could force a sale.

Domestic partnership laws can change some of these outcomes, but they vary widely not only from state to state but sometimes even by county or city. A handful of states such as California, the District of Columbia, Hawaii, Maine, Nevada, Oregon, Washington, Wisconsin, and New Jersey recognize domestic partnerships at the state level. Other states may allow them only in certain counties or municipalities. Because these rules differ so much, it is important to confirm what applies where you live and not assume that living together automatically grants, or denies, important legal rights

Whether your intent is to protect your children, grandchildren, a new partner, or a combination of all three, the key is to plan proactively so that your decisions determine what happens if you become incapacitated or after you're gone. Thoughtful legal planning ensures that the people you love are protected and that your wishes are honored without unnecessary conflict or confusion.

Living Separately

In some cases maintaining completely separate households is the cleanest solution. This approach allows both individuals to preserve financial independence, protect benefits, and avoid unintended tax consequences, while keeping their legal affairs neatly separated. It may not sound romantic at first, but for many older adults it provides the greatest sense of security while still leaving room for deep companionship and love.

We have had clients maintain their own homes and independence while nurturing long-term relationships with a companion. For some, this meant being able to keep pension or Social Security survivor benefits that would have been lost upon remarriage. For others, it eliminated the fear of commingling assets or losing control over what they had worked hard to build. And in nearly all cases, it reduced the potential for conflict between adult children and a parent's new partner.

Choosing to live separately does not diminish the relationship. It reframes it. By drawing clear boundaries, couples can focus on companionship and shared experiences without the stress of merging finances or navigating complex estate issues. For the right couple, this balance between independence and intimacy can create both peace of mind and a richer, more intentional connection in later life.

At the end of the day, this is a personal decision. Love can flourish in many forms. But knowing the rules and the risks means you can choose the path that best protects both your heart and your future.

Estate Planning with Remarriage

The goal of careful estate planning at this stage is beyond protecting your money. It's also about protecting your wishes, your relationships, and your future. It's about establishing clarity and compassion while making sure the people you care about aren't left to clean up a legal or financial mess during an already emotional time. Whether you choose to marry again, live together, or stay independent, a well-structured estate plan ensures that you, not the courts, remain in charge of what happens next.

And while it's important to protect the interests of children and grandchildren from a prior marriage, it's equally important to think about how your relationship may evolve over time. Many second marriages begin with careful attention to preserving assets for heirs, which is both reasonable and responsible. But life changes. Relationships deepen. As the years pass, the person who once entered your life as a new partner will hopefully become someone you've built a home, a history, and a life with. If your estate plan is rigidly structured to prioritize heirs without leaving room to care for your spouse, you may unintentionally create hardship, resentment, or even legal battles after you're gone.

Surviving his first wife, Jack remarried in his 80s. After selling his own home, he moved into hers, where they lived together for more than a decade. Over the years, Jack invested significant personal funds into improving the property, treating it as their shared home. But they didn't account for that in how the property was titled or in their estate plan. And when his second wife passed away, everything changed. Her daughter, determined to reclaim control, demanded that Jack leave. While he was briefly hospitalized, she took matters into her own hands. She changed the locks and barred him from reentering the home he had helped maintain and cherish. What followed was a painful and protracted legal battle. Family members were drawn into the conflict, and Jack, disoriented and grieving, was forced to fight for access to the only home he had known for years, all while navigating the emotional fallout of his wife's death. In the end, the money Jack had invested into the house flowed not to his own sons but to his wife's daughter, the very one who tried to force him out. That was a harsh outcome that could have been avoided with proper planning

That is also why it's critical to build flexibility into your planning, and to revisit your plan as the marriage grows. Protecting your heirs and protecting your spouse are not mutually exclusive goals, but they require thoughtful balancing. A living plan is one that reflects your current wishes, not just your intentions at the time of remarriage, and it ensures that you honor both your past and your present. Good estate planning is never one and done. It's a living reflection of the people and relationships that matter most to you.

The Importance of Prenuptial Agreements (and Postnuptial Agreements)

Prenuptial agreements are often misunderstood, especially later in life. Many people still think of a prenup as a signal of distrust, as if asking for one means you expect the relationship to fail. But nothing could be further from the truth. A well-crafted prenuptial agreement is not a prediction of failure. It's an act of protection, clarification, and respect for everyone involved. It allows two adults to be honest about their financial realities, their obligations to family, and their intentions for the future. It gives structure to what would otherwise be left to state laws and courts. Far from undermining a relationship, a good prenup can strengthen it by making sure that no one feels vulnerable, misled, or financially exposed as life unfolds.

One of the most important reasons to have a prenuptial agreement is to protect the legacy you've spent a lifetime building. It's not just for yourself, but for your children and grandchildren. If you remarry without a prenup, your new spouse could have automatic rights to a share of your estate, retirement accounts, or even business interests, regardless of your original intentions. Imagine, for example, that you and your former spouse built assets intended for your children that you had together. Without a prenup, those assets could end up split between your children and your new spouse's three adult children, reducing their share from 50 percent each to only 20 percent. Situations like this can create lasting conflict and leave your family with an outcome far different from what you intended

Remarriage without a prenup opens the door to elective share claims, commingling issues, and spousal inheritance rights. Consequently, a prenup gives you the ability to separate premarital assets, protect family inheritances, and clearly define how your estate will ultimately be distributed. Without it, you risk diluting the legacy you intended to pass on to future generations, creating confusion, resentment, and conflict among your heirs.

Blending finances without a clear agreement can also create unintentional harm during life, not just after death. Commingling assets, such as opening joint accounts, buying property together, or using shared income streams, can blur ownership lines in ways that make it difficult to protect what each person brought into the marriage. It can also expose one spouse to the debts, liabilities, or financial risks of the other. Without a prenuptial or postnuptial agreement clearly defining what is shared and what remains separate, well-meaning couples can inadvertently entangle themselves in financial situations they never intended. Careful planning doesn't diminish love; it gives it the foundation to grow without fear or confusion.

If you have already remarried without a prenuptial agreement, it's not too late to put protections in place. A postnuptial agreement, signed after marriage, can accomplish many of the same goals. You can focus on clarifying what assets remain separate, protect inheritances for children and grandchildren, and outline how property will be handled in the event of death or divorce. While postnups can be a little more sensitive to negotiate because the legal relationship is already in place, they are still a powerful tool for couples who want to align their financial intentions thoughtfully and avoid future misunderstandings. Whether through a prenup or postnup, the important thing is to recognize that clear agreements can bring peace of mind for everyone involved.

MANAGING FINANCES AS A COUPLE

One of the most important decisions you'll face after remarriage or forming a new partnership is how to manage your finances day-to-day. Should you merge your money? Keep it completely separate? Something in between? There's no one right answer, but setting clear financial expectations early is important to protecting both your relationship and your financial well-being.

Many couples choose a hybrid approach. They maintain separate accounts for personal spending while creating a joint account for shared household expenses like housing, utilities, travel, and groceries. This structure allows for transparency in managing the costs of living together, while preserving personal autonomy and reducing the potential for conflict over discretionary spending. Others keep finances entirely separate, treating each partner's assets and income independently, which can be particularly important when there are children or legacy goals involved from prior marriages.

Whatever structure you choose, the key is to be deliberate. Have open conversations early about how bills will be paid, how large purchases will be handled, and what financial support, if any, is expected or intended. Putting informal agreements into writing, even if just between yourselves, can prevent misunderstandings later. Especially in second marriages later in life, financial transparency isn't just about protecting assets, it's about protecting the trust and respect that form the foundation of your new life together. Clear financial agreements allow love to grow without the burden of unspoken expectations or hidden resentments.

BLENDED FAMILIES AND PLANNING

Blending families after loss is about more than just protecting assets. It is also about managing relationships with care. Financial planning in this situation often requires balancing different priorities. You may want to provide for a new spouse or partner while also preserving the legacy you intended for your children and grandchildren. The objective is to create a plan that respects your values, supports your relationships, and reduces the potential for conflict.

A strong plan does more than divide assets. It acknowledges the life you built before, reflects your current circumstances, and ensures that both past and present commitments are honored. The focus is not on choosing between your past and future, but on creating an approach that provides clarity and peace of mind for those you leave behind.

It is also important to recognize that not everyone may agree with your decisions. Adult children, for example, may struggle with a parent's choice to remarry, support a new partner, or reallocate resources. Sometimes kids may need financial help during their lifetime, such as assistance with education, a wedding, or a first home. Your plan should address these situations in a way that meets individual needs without undermining your broader estate strategy.

In many blended families, maintaining some financial separation can give each spouse the ability to honor prior commitments to children and extended family while keeping the new household stable. What matters most are clear boundaries, thoughtful planning, and open communication. Together, these steps can help protect both family relationships and financial intentions.

LONG-TERM CARE PLANNING AFTER LOSS: PROTECTING YOURSELF AND THE LIFE YOU'VE REBUILT

Long-term care planning is one of the most important and often overlooked pieces of rebuilding your retirement after loss. As a single retiree, you now bear the full responsibility for your future care needs. If you require assistance with daily activities, memory care, or nursing home support later in life, the emotional and financial burden falls squarely on your shoulders unless you plan ahead. Many people mistakenly believe that Medicare will cover long-term care, but it does not. Medicare only provides limited coverage for skilled nursing care after a hospitalization and does not pay for extended custodial care, which is the kind of help most people eventually need.

This reality makes planning essential. Long-term care costs can erode your savings, disrupt your independence, and limit your choices if you don't have a strategy in place. Long-term care encompasses a wide range of services, from basic help with daily activities like bathing, dressing, and eating to more advanced care such as assisted living, memory care, or full nursing home support. The risk of needing care increases significantly with age, and it often arrives unexpectedly, whether due to illness, injury, or cognitive decline. Without a plan, the rising costs of long-term care can drain your retirement savings, limit your ability to choose where and how you live, and threaten the independence you've worked a lifetime to protect. Planning ahead ensures that if the need arises, you will have options and, more importantly, control over how your care is managed.

Generally, your options to protect yourself financially from this risk include purchasing a traditional long-term care insurance policy, exploring a hybrid life insurance policy with a long-term care rider, or setting aside specific assets to self-insure. There is no one perfect answer, but doing nothing leaves you exposed at a stage of life when you deserve protection, stability, and dignity. The best plan is one that aligns with your financial capacity, your health status, your personal comfort with risk, and that acknowledges the real possibility that care may be needed.

If you later form a companionship or remarry, long-term care planning remains just as critical, but naturally the conversation expands. It's important to discuss and document who is responsible if health declines. Will each partner provide care for the other? Will each maintain separate resources or insurance policies? You see, without clear understanding caregiving responsibilities and financial costs can fall unevenly, creating unintended stress or hardship. Therefore, setting clear expectations and maintaining some financial independence can help protect both you and your partner while honoring the life you are building together, and without jeopardizing either person's security.

Long-term care planning is about preserving your freedom, maintaining your dignity, and ensuring that you continue to live life on your own terms—whether alone, with family, or with a new partner by your side.

PERMISSION TO DREAM AGAIN

Grief will always be part of your story, but it does not have to define what lies ahead. Retirement after loss marks both an ending and a beginning—the ending of the life you planned together, and the beginning of a future you now have the power to shape. There are still friendships to build, passions to rediscover, and new experiences to pursue. Hoping for more and working toward a full, meaningful life is not a betrayal of what you lost. It is a way of honoring the life and love you shared.

When you are ready, begin taking control of your future. That means being deliberate in every area of your life. Organizing your finances, structuring your savings and investments, updating your estate plan, and preparing for long-term care are not just practical tasks, they are acts of self-respect and self-protection. Planning gives you the freedom and confidence to move forward. You deserve to be the one shaping the next stage of your life, rather than simply reacting to circumstances.

Taking control of your future also means caring for yourself beyond the financial checklists. Rebuilding social connections, meeting new people, and staying open to new experiences are important steps. They may feel uncomfortable at first, but over time they help create the structure and rhythm of your new life. But of course this process does not happen all at once. Step by step though you will begin to find your footing again.

However, a meaningful future is not accidental. It is something you build with intention. Each decision and each action helps create a retirement and a future that reflects your strength and resilience. It does not need to be fast or perfect. It only needs to be yours. Focus not on what has been lost, but on everything still ahead and worth living for.

CONCLUSION: STANDING ON NEW GROUND

You did not choose this path, nor the title of widow or widower, and yet here you are, facing loss, grief, paperwork, and decisions no one ever wants to make. You have had to untangle a life built for two and find your footing as one. That is not small work. It is one of the hardest and most courageous jobs there is.

Let this be your permission to step fully into the life ahead. Not a life defined by loss, but one shaped by everything you still have to live for. Widowhood forces you to face decisions you never imagined making alone, yet being the decision-maker does not mean you have to walk the path by yourself. Surround yourself with people you trust. Lean on their guidance to help carry the weight, protect what you are building, and give you the confidence to move forward. Your life is about more than merely surviving. It is about living with purpose, drawing strength from your past, and creating a future that reflects your resilience, your values, and above all your love.

This book was intended to help you see the decisions ahead not as an impossible mountain, but as a series of steps you can take at your own pace, with the right support. You have already begun that process. Each action you take marks the beginning of reclaiming your life. Standing on new ground does not mean letting go of what was. It means honoring it while protecting what you built together and shaping what now belongs to you alone. It means creating a future that reflects your priorities and your deepest values, even if it looks different from the one you originally planned.

You are allowed to look forward. You are allowed to seek joy again, to rebuild, to rest, and to grow. The work you have done—emotionally, financially, and legally—has laid a foundation that is strong enough to carry you. What comes next is yours to shape. You are not starting over. You are continuing on with more wisdom, more strength, and an even clearer understanding of what matters most.

This next chapter is yours to write. There are lives to touch, moments to savor, and a future still waiting for you to claim.

Author's Note and Next Steps

If this book has helped you feel a little more grounded, a little more prepared, or even just a little more understood, then it has done its job. You have carried a heavy weight, and I hope these pages have lightened the load in some small but meaningful way.

You are not alone in this. Many men and women find themselves navigating the same questions you are asking now—about security, independence, family, legacy, and the quiet but powerful question of *what now ?* My work is devoted to walking alongside those rebuilding their lives in retirement, moving forward with strength, faith, and grace.

If you would like to take the next step, I invite you to reach out, whether you are looking for trusted guidance, professional planning, or simply a place to begin a deeper conversation about your financial future. You can visit my website at longevitycapitalmgmt.com, explore available resources at retirerightseries.com, or schedule a time to talk. There is no pressure—only support, if and when you are ready.

Thank you for letting me be part of this time in your life. It is a privilege to have walked beside you in these pages as you move toward the life ahead.

With respect and care,
Terri McGray, Founder and President
Longevity Capital Management

Resources and Tools

These resources are designed to help you take action at your own pace, with clarity and confidence. Use them as needed, return to them when ready, and know that support is always within reach.

Additional resources, tools, and educational offerings are available online and will continue to expand over time. You can find the most current materials, along with optional courses and support, at www.retirerightseries.com.

1. The "Should Something Happen" Organizer

A printable and fillable guide to help you document final wishes, household instructions, personal items of sentimental value, and other non-legal details that matter deeply.

→ Download at: www.retirerightseries.com

2. Estate Plan Review Checklist

Use this to review your existing documents and identify what may need to be updated after the loss of a spouse. It includes trust and will updates, power of attorney review, titling review, and beneficiary audit

→ Download at: www.retirerightseries.com

3. Questions to Ask a Financial Advisor or Attorney

A list of thoughtful, practical questions to ask when interviewing a new advisor or attorney. Know what to expect and how to find someone who fits your needs.

→ Download at: www.retirerightseries.com

4. Recommended Reading

"Option B" by Sheryl Sandberg is a #1 *New York Times* Best Seller

After the sudden death of her husband, Sheryl Sandberg felt certain that she and her children would never feel pure joy again. Option B combines Sheryl's personal insights beginning with the gut-wrenching moment when she finds her husband, Dave Goldberg, collapsed on a gym floor, Sheryl opens up her heart—and her journal—to describe the acute grief and isolation she felt in the wake of his death. But Option B goes beyond Sheryl's loss to explore how a broad range of people have overcome hardships including illness, job loss, sexual assault, natural disasters, and the violence of war. Their stories reveal the capacity of the human spirit to persevere . . . and to rediscover joy.

"The Year of Magical Thinking" by Joan Didion is a *New York Times* Bestseller and National Book Award Winner

A stunning book of electric honesty and passion that explores an intensely personal yet universal experience: a portrait of a marriage—and a life, in good times and bad, that will speak to anyone who has ever loved a husband or wife or child.

5. Support Communities

National Grief Support Groups for Spousal Loss

Losing a spouse is a profound loss, but you don't have to navigate it alone. Below are well-established, active, and inclusive

US organizations that specialize in supporting widows and widowers.

Soaring Spirits International—*soaringspirits.org*
Soaring Spirits International (SSI) connects widowed people with each other. SSI's mission is to ensure that no one who is widowed needs to grieve in isolation, offering a range of peer support programs. Its signature event is *Camp Widow®*, an uplifting weekend retreat held multiple times a year in various US cities, where widowed men and women can meet others who understand and attend workshops on healing and rebuilding life after loss.

Modern Widows Club—*modernwidowsclub.org*
Modern Widows Club (MWC) is a community by and for widows (primarily women who have lost a spouse) with a focus on not just grief support but also personal growth. MWC offers a mix of local and virtual support.

The W Connection—*widowsconnection.org*
The W Connection is a national network created by women to help women rebuild their lives after the loss of a spouse. It is entirely peer-led and geared toward practical coping skills and mutual encouragement.

Hope for Widows Foundation—*hopeforwidows.org*
Hope for Widows Foundation is a national nonprofit formed to create a caring community for widowed women. It is run by widows and provides a safe, supportive space for women to heal after losing a husband or wife. It is completely online-based (there are no physical chapters), which allows widows from all over the US—and even internationally—to connect virtually and access resources.

National Widowers' Organization—*nationalwidowers.org*
The National Widowers' Organization (NWO) is created to support men grieving the loss of a spouse or partner. It arose from the recognition that men often grieve differently and have fewer outlets to talk about their emotions.

Widowers Support Network—*widowerssupportnetwork.com*
Widowers Support Network (WSN) is a worldwide support community for men who have lost their spouses, founded by widower and author Herb Knoll. While not a nonprofit charity, its mission is very much service-oriented: to *provide a "brotherhood through loss"* where widowers can find others who truly understand what they're going through.

Tragedy Assistance Program for Survivors (TAPS)—*taps.org*
TAPS is a renowned national nonprofit that provides compassionate care for *all those grieving the death of a military service member or veteran.* This includes surviving spouses, but also children, parents, siblings, battle buddies—any relation. TAPS is especially significant for military widows and widowers, as it offers a broad, structured support network alongside others who have lost a loved one in military service.

American Widow Project (AWP)—*americanwidowproject.org*
AWP is a smaller but notable nonprofit that specifically focuses on young military widows. It was founded in 2007 by Taryn Davis, who lost her husband in Iraq, as a way to connect with other women who faced the sudden loss of a spouse in the military. AWP's motto is about unifying, educating, and empowering military widows, and honoring the legacy of their spouses.

WHERE TO BEGIN: HOW TO FIND THE RIGHT SUPPORT

If you're not sure where to start, here are some ways to find the right emotional support—based on what feels right for you:

For Professional Therapists and Grief Counselors

- PsychologyToday.com—A searchable database where you can filter by specialty (grief, trauma, loss), insurance coverage, and location.
- Grief.com—Offers resources and articles and often lists local and virtual support options.
- The American Counseling Association (counseling.org)—Provides tools to help you understand your options and locate licensed professionals.
- BetterHelp or Talkspace—Online platforms that offer virtual counseling, which can be especially helpful if you live in a rural area or prefer to talk from home.

For Grief Support Groups:

- Hospice organizations—Many offer free bereavement groups open to the community, whether or not your spouse was in their care. Try Hospice Foundation of America (hospicefoundation.org).
- Local hospitals—Many medical centers host or sponsor grief groups and can connect you to licensed facilitators.
- Churches and synagogues—Many faith communities offer free or donation-based groups, sometimes tailored to widows and widowers.
- The Dougy Center—Originally focused on childhood grief, they also provide guidance for adult loss and resources for families.

For Spiritual Support

- Clergy members—Whether or not you're actively part of a religious community, many pastors, priests, rabbis, and other spiritual leaders are open to offering support, guidance, or simply a listening ear. Their training often includes helping people navigate loss, doubt, and emotional overwhelm.
- Hospital or hospice chaplains—These professionals are trained to support people of all (or no) faiths and often have a deep understanding of grief.
- Faith-based counseling centers—Many communities have Christian, Jewish, or interfaith counseling groups with licensed professionals who integrate spirituality into the healing process.

Tips for Pursuing Emotional Support

- Give yourself permission to try one conversation. You're not committing to a lifetime of therapy. Just start with one call, one session.
- Don't wait until you feel "ready." The support often helps you become ready.
- If someone doesn't feel like the right fit, try someone else. This is not failure; it's discernment.
- You don't need to be in crisis to ask for help. Just feeling alone or uncertain is reason enough.

Support doesn't always show up in the form of friends or family. Sometimes it arrives through a stranger who knows how to listen and how to help you carry what feels too heavy to hold on your own.

Acknowledgments

This book would not have been possible without the contributions and support of many individuals.

I am grateful to my editor Jon Harrison and designer and publishing professional Susan Shankin, who helped shape this work with care, precision, and respect for the subject matter. Their expertise strengthened both the clarity and the integrity of the finished work.

I also want to acknowledge my team, whose professionalism, dedication, and commitment to serving clients at the highest level make this work possible every day. Their work, along with the insights shared by many colleagues and professionals over the years, has helped refine my understanding of the financial and emotional complexities that accompany widowhood.

Most importantly, I am deeply grateful to the clients and widows who have placed their trust in me over many decades, through both strong and challenging markets. Their confidence in my work and my guidance has never been taken lightly. Their questions, concerns, and lived experiences, shared with honesty and resilience, are the foundation of this book.

Finally, I am grateful for the personal support that made this work possible, especially from my husband, Paul, who understood the quiet persistence required to see it through. I am equally grateful to my daughters, Jaclyn, Madison, and Cody, whose encouragement and steady support mean more to me than they know. I also thank my mother, whose belief in me never wavered. Their presence and support are a constant source of strength.

About the Author

Terri McGray, CFP®, AIF®, is the founder and president of Longevity Capital Management, a boutique advisory firm focused on retirement and longevity planning. She began working in the industry in 1988 and has spent more than three decades helping individuals navigate the financial decisions that arise as life transitions from accumulation to income.

Over the course of her career, Terri has guided clients through multiple market cycles, changing tax environments, and periods of heightened uncertainty. Her work centers on aligning investment strategy with real world income needs, longevity risk, and life transitions, with a particular focus on helping clients avoid forced decisions during vulnerable periods.

Terri leads her firm's investment philosophy and planning process, emphasizing thoughtful preparation, disciplined execution, and strategies designed to adapt as circumstances change. She is the author of the Retire Right series and a frequent speaker on retirement planning, longevity, and financial decision making.

She lives and works in California and serves clients nationwide.

For more information,
please visit www.longevitycapitalmgmt.com.

www.ingramcontent.com/pod-product-compliance
Lightning Source LLC
LaVergne TN
LVHW090348240926
848801LV00017B/183/J